THE ALCHEMY OF ZEN

THE ALCHEMY OF ZEN

OSHO'S INSIGHTS ON CONSCIOUS LIVING

SWAMI CHAITANYA KEERTI

wisdom tree

ISBN: 978-81-8328-120-1

Published by
Wisdom Tree
4779/23 Ansari Road
Darya Ganj
New Delhi-110002
Ph.: 23247966/67/68

Published by Shobit Arya for Wisdom Tree; *edited by* Manju Gupta; *designed by* Kamal P. Jammual; *typeset at* Marks & Strokes, New Delhi-110002 and *printed at* Print Perfect, New Delhi-110064

Introduction

Swami Chaitanya Keerti became a disciple of Osho, the enlightened spiritual master, in the early seventies and has ever since been extensively involved with the media — as spokesperson for Osho Commune International in Pune for many years, founder and former editor of *Osho Times International*, editor of *Osho World Magazine*, editor and publisher of Osho books and a prolific writer with several compilations in his name. He is presently the spokesperson of Osho World Foundation, based in New Delhi. I have been privileged to be his friend and fellow-traveller for more than 30 years.

Swami Keerti's latest endeavour is this compilation of individual articles he wrote for various newspapers and magazines over the past five years or so. During that period he conducted meditation workshops throughout India and several Asian countries, sharing his perception and humour with a multitude of seekers and meditators. Inspired by their questions, current affairs and mundane day-to-day observations, he balanced Osho's teachings and his own understanding in a remarkable mix of an insightful art of living, mysticism, anecdotes and wit.

This book has a lot to offer to the spiritual seeker as well as to the merely curious onlooker. Open the book at random and you will immediately be enthralled by the write-up on a very familiar topic but rendered here with a different vision than you would expect. Swami Keerti not only chats intimately with the reader, but also offers sound advice on how to improve one's awareness, meditativeness and consciousness in life. He blends excerpts from discourses given by Osho to highlight the various issues about love and reality, meditation and consciousness, spirituality and celebration, life and death.

Osho once said, "To be an Indian has nothing to do with geography; it has something to do with an inner approach towards reality. Modern India has forgotten the ways of the Buddha, and has forgotten how to live with Buddhas. I am trying to reveal that treasure to you again. Let it sink deep in your heart. The first principle is the art of living. Be life-affirmative. Life is synonymous with God. You can drop the word God — 'life is God'. Live with reverence, with great respect and gratitude. You have not earned this life; it is a sheer gift from the beyond. Feel thankful and prayerful, and take as many bites of it as possible and chew it before digesting it well. Make your life an aesthetic experience. And not much is needed to make it an aesthetic experience; just an aesthetic consciousness, a sensitive soul is enough. Become more sensitive, more sensuous, and you will become more spiritual."

September 2007 Bhagawati Morriss

Contents

EVERYDAY ZEN

永恒

Zen says: This is all. There is no other life; there is no other existence. This ordinary existence is beautiful. There is no need for any other world; this world is more than enough. Zen is the greatest alchemy. It transforms your ordinary, mundane life into a sacred, holy life.

Lovely Zen

Pour your whole being into everything and life will become a meditation.

In another article in this book it is explained how living could be about meditation, because meditation is not something separate from life. Life without meditation is not meaningful. Meditation makes it richer. In other words, meditation can be described as a way of life, in all its richness and fruitfulness.

I would like to explain this through a lovely Zen anecdote. There was a great Zen master in Japan; I don't remember his name. Anyway, masters are beyond names: a nameless consciousness. This Zen master had a very beautiful *ashram* in a deep forest. The king of the country came to see him. He was very curious to know why this master had become so famous and what his teachings were. As the king entered the *ashram*, he saw a man chopping wood. The king went to him and asked him where the Zen master lived. The man continued chopping wood as if nobody had disturbed him. Interrupting again, the king enquired: "Please sir, could you guide me to the master of this *ashram*?"

The man stopped chopping the wood and looked at the king. He replied: "Over there you see a hut, that's the master's hut. Just go there and wait for the master. He will come out to see you."

The king turned towards the hut and waited there. A little later, the Zen master, in his beautiful attire, appeared before the king. To his amazement, the king saw that it was the same person whom he had seen chopping wood. Witnessing the king's astonishment, the master said to him: 'You are surprised, aren't you? Yes, I am the same man you saw when you entered the *ashram*. I was doing my work-meditation and I was so absorbed in that act, that I did not even notice you at first. I was pouring my whole being into that ordinary act, but my totality had made it so extraordinary. It is the first lesson in Zen teaching to you: Be total in whatever you do. Had your act of seeing me become total, you too would have glimpsed meditation there and then. But you missed it. Any action, it doesn't matter what, done in its totality becomes meditation. Be in the moment wherever you are and you won't need any other mode of meditation, because meditation is not a doing; it is your being.

After this conversation, the Zen master offered the king a cup of tea.

The king was grateful. Taking the cup in his hand, he kept looking at the master. The master reminded him: "Look at the cup of tea. Hold it in such a way that there's nothing else in the world to do. Forget all your spiritual questions; just drink your tea. Now it is the most spiritual act that you can do. Drink and don't think. Feel this aroma spreading around you. Let your whole being become one with this act of sipping tea — each sip is awareness.

Then the master held another cup of tea in his own hands — with such grace that no other emperor on earth could match that grace. In that moment, even the king looked like a beggar in front of the master.

Unawareness is poverty. Awareness is richness — the real inner wealth.

Zen is spreading like wild fire around the world, because

it's the purest form of meditation. Zen brings total awareness to any activity and it becomes divine; it becomes real creativity. That's why Zen appeals to all.

It is not a religion, it is a way of life. A lifestyle.

Welcome to Zen.

Silver Magic of the Full Moon

A full-moon night is the best time for meditation, when the noises of the day give way to the silence of the night. Open your heart and let your eyes be filled with the moon's nectar. Absorb this nectar into your whole being. Feel the coolness and tenderness.

Let this atmosphere be metamorphosed into an *atma*-sphere, the soul-space. Let your body sway or dance gently, and bring yourself into the realm of grace. The more you melt, the more you can move upward into the vast sky of consciousness.

We carry within us both the mountains and valleys. We can climb high and feel on top of the world, reaching the Everest of our consciousness. We could also feel down in the dumps as if we are in a Black Hole. Human consciousness can throw us into the dark dismal ditches, or it can help us open our wings, sending us soaring high into the sky.

Consciousness is a liquid phenomenon and so is the moon's energy. Its powerful presence in the sky resonates in our inner sky of consciousness. It affects our psyche.

In his discourse, 'Celebrate Myself: God is Nowhere, Life is Now Here', Osho says: "The full moon night has a specialness that is now being recognised by science. But scientists approach it from the wrong side, because they are living on the wrong side of the earth; in the West. They become aware that more murders are committed on full-moon nights, more suicides happen, more people go insane... The full-moon night affects the ocean — waves become tidal, as if the ocean is trying to reach out to the moon."

Man consists of 80 per cent water, so something in him also starts feeling a subtle vibration. Scientists say man is the other end of the evolutionary process — in the beginning was the fish. So we have a deep connection.

Osho says: "We carry great potential of which we are utterly unaware. It is painful to break that hard shell (of ignorance), but once you are ready to go through the pain, and once the shell is broken, life takes a quantum leap. You become immortal. You are no more in darkness; you become a full moon night. And you know misery no more. Bliss simply becomes your nature, your very existence."

Osho adds: "The moon represents the most blissful and beautiful phenomenon. One can become that beauty, that splendour. It is within our reach, for we can hold the moon in our hearts. Going to the moon is useless. Far more significant is the process of bringing the moon in."

Osho explains: "The moon creates magic every night. It simply reflects the sun's rays, functioning only as a mirror. The master, too, is a mirror, and meditation makes you a mirror — clean and pure, so everything is reflected in you as it is — devoid of judgement."

The moon, just by reflecting them, transforms the hot rays of the sun into cool energy. As a master, he absorbs the same energy that you absorb; he eats the same food as you eat; he drinks the same water, he breathes the same air, but some alchemical change is constantly going on in him.

On a full-moon night of every month, Zen practitioners watch the moon all through the night. And as they continue witnessing the moon, a deep tranquillity and silence descends over them, particularly on the night when Gautama, the Buddha was born, became enlightened, and died. So this is a special night for Zen Buddhists.

Slowing Down with Zen

Enjoy one's own company – that is the secret of Zen.

A disciple asked a Zen master: "What is the greatest miracle in the world?"

The master replied: "To sit here all by myself."

We have heard of all kinds of miracles, but meditation is the greatest miracle possible. There can be no bigger miracle than it: sitting by yourself. We always seek company. We always engage or occupy ourselves, going from one occupation to another, without a gap. If we are bored with newspapers, we switch on the television. If television doesn't satisfy us, we log on to the Internet, start chatting without any purpose. We seek any garbage anywhere, in the name of entertainment. But we do not sit by ourselves. Nobody wants to meet their own self; everybody is interested in meeting others.

Meeting oneself, or it is more appropriate to say, being oneself, sitting by oneself, is the most arduous thing. That is why the Zen master says that it is the greatest miracle in the world. Sitting by oneself is real meditation. We should call it *dhyan*. The word 'meditation' is not the right translation of *dhyan*. Meditation means meditating upon something, while *dhyan* means being aware, awakened, not focused on anything outside us; not thinking or contemplating about any object or our personal God. It is pure awareness and nothing else.

It is not about concentrating on anything. Just being centred and being by yourself — that is *dhyan*.

This word travelled from India to China with the first Buddhist master, Bodhidharma, and took the form of *chan*. So it was pronounced as *chan* in China. Later it went from China to Japan and the original Hindi word *dhyan* was pronounced there as *zan*. And finally it was called Zen in Japan. Now it has become famous all over the world because the teachings of Buddha have tremendous appeal in the West. Dalai Lama is a rage in the West. But serious meditators, who are not much into political activities or social reform, have become interested in Zen. There are more schools of Zen in USA than in India. In India, Zen is more well known as a car. It all depends on the needs or development of a country. Evidently, India needs cars more than *dhyan* or meditation. Japan and the US already have more cars than they need. Now what they need is freedom from speed; they want to stop for a while and meditate. That is why Zen has so much appeal there. While this appeal grows there, India will be looking for new modes of speed before it stops to find time for meditation. Let me remind you that sitting by yourself is not loneliness. In loneliness you miss others. It means you enjoy being alone and you don't need the presence of any person who can give you joy. You are contented and it doesn't matter whether the other person is there or not. 'Aloneness' is a blissful state of consciousness and this is the miracle of Zen.

The Heart of Zen

Generally it is believed that meditation, *dhyan* or Zen has nothing to do with emotions, feelings and the heart. Actually, this is not true. Zen is not such a dry affair. Zen is always throbbing with a heart. It may not have anything to do with your IQ, but it has much to do with your EQ — Emotional Quotient.

Zen attracts intellectuals as they think that Zen is all about the mind involving an intellectual attitude. No, it is not. Zen is actually no-mind; it is passion and compassion — passion for the impossible and compassion for all beings. Zen is the heart of Buddha, who is known as *Kalyanmitra.*

Once there was a great Zen master who had an equally great disciple, Rinzai, who was more well known than even his master. His fame had spread all over Japan. He came when the Zen master died and thousands of people gathered at the funeral. They were all shocked to see that Rinzai was crying like an ordinary person. Now that is just not done. A monk or someone who meditates is not supposed to cry; instead he is expected to be beyond such attachments. The people asked Rinzai, "Why all this crying? What would people think when they see the chief disciple of a great Zen master shedding tears? Do you still have an attachment to the physical body of the master? Have you not gone beyond all these worldly attachments? Or are you still not enlightened?"

Rinzai replied, "Who fed you with all this nonsense that enlightened people cannot cry? I see the tears rolling down. And I do know that the soul is immortal, only the body dies. And I know that my master was not merely a body. And he has not gone anywhere — he has become a presence without a body. But my heart cries because my eyes are missing the lovely presence of a body that carried his soul so beautifully. The body is a temple of the Divine. My eyes are missing that temple"

He continued, "Don't look at life intellectually or logically. Life is more than logic. Life is love. Life is laughter. Life brings tears also. Life consists of all these feelings. It is not dry; it is very colourful. Enjoy all the colours of life just as a witness.

Rinzai added, "Life is not a dull affair — it is to be lived in intensity, totality. These are just some other names of life. Accept life. Embrace life. Be one with it. Only by being one with it can you witness it. People say that Buddha never laughed. Nothing can be falser than that. Zen and Tao traditions had to create the laughing Buddha just to remind us that he laughed. But we tend to be very serious and accept anything that is very serious. We are impressed by the sight of an ascetic torturing himself in the scorching sun by the roadside. We touch his feet, thinking that here is somebody who does not care about his body. And we deride ourselves for being slaves of the body. But we forget that one who is not compassionate towards his own body cannot be compassionate to others. With meditation come compassion and love. And the nearest object of your love and compassion has to be your own body. Keep your body healthy and vibrant, as this is the first and foremost meditation.

Followers of Zen say, "This very body is the Buddha; this very earth, the lotus paradise."

The Mad Act

In his book, *You Can Win*, a famous motivational speaker, Shiv Khera, writes: Dr Karl Menninger, a world-renowned psychiatrist, was once asked, "What would you advise a person if you knew that he was going to have a nervous breakdown?"

Menninger gave an unusual reply, "I would advise the person to lock his home, go to the other side of the town, find someone in need and help that person. By doing this we get out of our own way."

'Get out of your own way,' is a Zen saying. What Menninger suggests is also a Zen method to cure madness or insanity. But he has tried to improve upon the method and by doing this, he has corrupted the method a bit. There can be no improvement on Zen methods, because they are not psychological methods. The realm of psychology is far below the realm of Zen. Psychology indulges in the long-drawn process of analysis, going round in circles. Zen is a vertical journey and moves like an arrow to hit the target. It functions with surgical precision. Zen is the purest science of transformation. It is a common practice in Zen monasteries to isolate an person insane and give him a private room, away from the main area. For a few days the person is left to himself. He has the freedom to be himself. Nobody is there to judge him or force him to do anything. He is just left alone to throw out his madness into the void. Living like this for some days is a natural cure.

The biggest problem that we face in society is that people do not give each other enough space. We intrude upon each other's space. All our relationships are like this — be it a parent-child relationship or that between spouses. Though our intentions may be good, such an attitude creates a lot of irritation.

In such suffocating situations, we keep accumulating madness. But we are not allowed to express it in public. We fear judgement. 'What will people think? Am I mad?' We keep on pushing down this madness into our subconscious mind, suppressing it in the basement of our mind. And one day when we can no longer tolerate this poison inside, we explode — mostly on others. Usually, it is the same people with whom we have been behaving well. We end up showing them our ugly face. This is the story of all of us — we hide behind our social masks.

Zen teaches us to unmask ourselves and find our original face. Zen has nothing to do with morality; it has everything to do with originality. The end result is the real morality that emerges out of pure consciousness; not out of our behaviour or social conduct or the hypocrisy of the society.

Transmission of Light in Deep Silence

Why did Bodhidharma, the greatest Zen master, go from India to China? This question has been posed repeatedly in the Zen schools of thought all over the world.

He could not find anybody in India to whom he could transmit his enlightenment. There were scholars, pundits and philosophers available, but to them the transmission of enlightenment was not possible, as this happens only in the deepest silence. This experience can be transferred from the master to the disciple who has dissolved into silence — it is only silence and silence alone. The scholars and pundits are not silent people — they are full of words; they blah blah... endlessly. With them it is a psychological need; indeed a disease.

A young man confessed his sins to a priest thus: "Sure, Father, I had sex seven times last night."

The priest asked: "How many women?"

"Ah, Father, there was only one woman," answered Pat.

To which the priest said: "Well, it is not as bad as I thought. Who is the woman?"

"My wife, Father."

"Well," said the priest, "there is nothing wrong with that, Son."

"I know, Father, but I just had to tell someone," replied Pat.

Osho explains: "There are moments when you just have to tell someone. If you don't talk about it, it becomes heavy on you. If you talk, you are released and relaxed. If you can find a sympathetic listener, good; otherwise just talk to yourself. But don't repress it; if repressed, it will become a burden on you. Just sit in front of the wall and have a good talk. In the beginning you will find it a little crazy, but the more you do it, the more you will see the beauty of it. It is less violent. It does not waste somebody else's time, and it works the same way; it does the same. You are relieved. And after a good talk with the wall, you will feel very, very relaxed. In fact, everybody needs to do it. The world would be better and more silent if people start talking to the walls. Try it. It will be deep meditation — knowing well that the wall is not listening. But that is not the point.

Zen master Bodhidharma also used to sit facing the wall. After nine years of sitting he found a disciple who was worthy of the transmission of enlightenment. As they say in Hindi — *jyoti se jyoti jaley*. Enlightenment from the master to the disciple is just like the transmission of light, which happens in the deepest silence.

The Mathematics of Opportunity Cost

Let the mind not oscillate between many choices. According to the Advaita, real health comes from wholeness or non-duality.

There is an interesting story in the life of the great master, Hakuin. He was honoured by his neighbours for leading a pure life. One day it was discovered that a beautiful girl, who lived near Hakuin's hut, was pregnant. The parents were very angry. At first the girl would not reveal who the father was, but after much persuasion, she named Hakuin.

In great anger the parents went to Hakuin, but all he would say was, "Is that so?" After the child was born, it was taken to Hakuin, who had lost his reputation by this time. He took great care of the child. He obtained from his neighbours things like milk, food and everything else the child needed.

A year later, the girl-mother could stand it no longer, so she told her parents the truth — the real father was a young man who worked in a fish market. They went to Hakuin to apologise and ask for his forgiveness and get the child back.

The master willingly gave the child away, saying, "Is that so?"

Such problems are encountered not only by Zen masters, but happen to all of us. Life is so mysterious that all of us land up in misunderstandings. There's confusion at every step and there are unavoidable situations, difficult to deal with. And it happens that our choices and preferences don't always work. Sometimes these choices and preferences lead to greater complications. In such a situation, we are always in a dilemma about what to choose and what not to. We can choose one thing and soon realise that we have made a wrong choice. Then we choose something else and again realise that it is no better.

We keep oscillating between the many choices given by our mind such that our misery does not end with our choices. In this process we never realise that there's something wrong with our mind, which is always choosing the opposite. It is never satisfied with what it chooses; discontentment is its very nature. Give it something very precious and soon you will see that the thing is no longer as precious; it has become ordinary and undesirable.

Our mind, which is always seeking something new and has strong preferences, is leading us astray. It is not in the nature of the mind to be happy with whatever it gets. It will complain. Soon it will find something wrong with it and start running for something else.

That's the way we lose touch with the present moment and start imagining about the future. Our preferences destroy our 'present' for the 'future'. Our reality is sacrificed on the altar of imagination. We need to look deeply into the nature of our mind, penetrate into it without paying attention to the choices it offers us, without swaying with its preferences. By observing our mind we will reach a state of consciousness, which gives us clarity and wholeness of vision.

Sosan, the great Zen master, says: "The great way is not difficult for those who have no preferences."

It is difficult for our mind to understand that one can live without preferences. It is unconceivable for us that even Nature — trees, birds, animals, rivers, mountains, planets — is moving with the natural flow of existence without any preferences. It is only man who faces difficulties. And where does this difficulty come from? It comes from his mind.

The mind is a great divider, an arbitrator of what is good and what is bad and what is right and what is wrong. Give your mind anything and soon you will see that it creates a duality. First, it divides everything and then it creates conflicts between the divided parts. And it is amazing that it tries to solve the conflicts created by itself. This soon becomes a vicious circle.

It is similar to the fact that the disease gives us the cure for the ailment, telling us the ways and means to stay healthy. But things become even more complicated. Talking about the Eastern and the Western approaches, Osho explains: "The mind is a disease. This is a basic truth the East has discovered. The West says the mind can become ill or can be healthy. Western psychology depends on two realities — it can be healthy or ill. But the East says the mind as such is the disease, it cannot be healthy. No amount of psychiatry will help; at the most you can make it normally ill. The East says that the very nature of the mind is such that it will remain unhealthy. The word 'health' is beautiful. It comes from the same root as the word 'whole'. Health, healing, whole, holy — they all come from the same root."

Sages of the East are in agreement about this nature of the mind and they have advised us to meditate and go beyond the mind, to transcend it, to be in the realm of witnessing consciousness — what Lord Krishna and Sage Ashtavakra term as *sakshin*, or what the modern mystic J. Krishnamurti calls 'choiceless awareness, non-judgemental consciousness'. The mind is a phenomenon of choice, and Osho proclaims:

"You choose and you are in misery. Choose and you are in the trap, because whenever you choose, you choose something against something else. If you are for something, you must be against something; you cannot be only for and you cannot be only against. When the 'for' enters, the 'against' follows as a shadow."

When you choose, you divide. Then you say, "This is good and this is wrong." And life is unity. Existence remains undivided; existence remains in deep unison. This is the natural Advaita, the non-duality, the real health that comes from oneness and wholeness.

The Secret Alchemy of *Yin* and *Yang*

Life exists in relation to the complementarity of opposites and is expressed as *yin* and *yang*. According to Tao, all things are either female *(yin)* or male *(yang)* in Nature. *Yin* and *yang* together make up the wholeness of the universe. They breathe meaning into each other. Light cannot exist without darkness. Action is impossible without the background of inaction. One's being depends on doing; doing on being. Just being makes you lazy; just doing makes you hyper. This is what has been happening to the East and the West. The East has become lazy and fatalistic by believing that everything happens on its own, like a child growing in the womb. This is a feminine approach of waiting and waiting. The East, in the past, represented such feminine qualities, while the West went the other way. It became too active, conquered Nature, went ballistic. The whole world suffered because of this aggression. The root cause of suffering is the imbalance in the male and female qualities in the world.

Osho talks about how different the worlds of men and women are, and how difficult it is for them to understand each other. The past has been full of misunderstandings, but the future doesn't have to be. He says: "If all differences between men and women disappear, then the polarity will go away. Men and women are like negative and positive poles — they are attracted magnetically. Hence, conflict is natural. But through understanding, compassion, love and empathy, any problem can be solved. Man needs as much liberation as woman. Both need liberation from the mind. They should cooperate and help each other to get liberated."

In *My Way: The Way of the White Clouds*, Osho says: "Once you know this secret alchemy of using the opposites, the contradictory, you are free. Otherwise, you create inner imprisonments. There are people who say, 'How can I do this? I have never done this.' Just the other day there was somebody who said to me, 'How can I do active meditation, because for many years I have been sitting silently?' He had chosen, and he has reached nowhere. Otherwise there was no need to come to me. But he cannot meditate because he has adopted an inactive posture. This is getting frozen."

Osho adds: "Become more of a movement. Keep moving and allow life to flow. Once you know that balance is possible between the opposites, once you have a glimpse of it, then you know the art. Then everywhere in life, in every dimension, you can attain that balance easily. Once you know the knack of it, whatsoever you do, the balance follows you like a shadow."

ART OF MEDITATION

永恒

Meditation is the only real alchemy. All else that goes on being written in the name of alchemy is just bullshit, occult nonsense, esoteric rubbish. The true science consists of only one thing — that is meditation, because that is the bridge from the body to consciousness. Once you have reached your centre of being and once you have known that you are consciousness, you are beyond birth, beyond death.

And when one is beyond time, great joy arises because all fears disappear, all darkness disappears.

The Alchemy of Meditation

There are two ways of living life — consciously or mechanically, robot-like or with full awareness.

Most people live their life in a half-drowsy state, moving semi-consciously. That's why we see so much misery and anguish around ourselves. People don't know how to act with full consciousness. They simply react unconsciously or mechanically. We press an electric button and the fan is turned on. Similarly someone presses our 'button' and we start reacting instantly.

Someone calls us names or insults us, we become furious and want to kill him. This behaviour cannot be called conscious or meditative behaviour. It is simply mechanical, creating a chain reaction in all of us and making us chained. It is bondage; not freedom.

Mediation is a science, a pure science of awareness — to be free. Meditation is freedom. Meditation is watchfulness, witnessing each act that we do. Meditation is a way of life in which we transform ourselves from a baser metal to gold. It's an alchemical process to bring about an inner metamorphosis. It's a revolution in the individual and ultimately a revolution in the society. One awakened being who goes through this revolution becomes a Buddha, the Enlightened One, who shows light to millions of people for thousands of years. It's the magic of meditation. What one Buddha does is incomparable; thousands of social reformers are not capable of doing that. Social reformers bring changes only superficially; these are cosmetic reforms. But Buddha brings transformation deep within. That's the science of meditation.

The future belongs to such a science. Science is universal — that which is applicable to all. Beliefs and systems are not universal; they are local or parochial in nature. You can argue or fight about them. They lead us nowhere. They don't lead to self-realisation. Meditation is an inward journey into the unknown treasures that we carry within us — the joy and bliss that's within us. A blissful person, an illumined person, brings joy and light to others. He is a blessing, a benediction.

In this book, I will share with you some methods of meditation — how we can become more conscious and aware and how we can live our life, in a more healthy, more joyful, manner.

Laughter is a Form of Meditation

Osho's greatest gift to humanity is to teach a lifestyle of meditation and celebration. He does not want man to renounce his life and escape to the Himalayas, but remain in the marketplace and learn the art of meditation to transform this life into one of playful creativity.

Man should not take this life as a burden, but treat it as a unique gift from existence. The gift transcends religious seriousness and monotony, enabling us to expand beyond the limits of our intellect. This is an art of living, which the modern man must inculcate.

Osho introduces laughter as meditation. Our noisy mind stops for a few precious moments when we laugh spontaneously, giving us the taste of meditation.

In one of his discourses on 'The Transmission of the Lamp', Osho says: "One of my contributions to religion is a sense of humour which no other religion contains. And one of my basic statements about it is that laughter is the highest spiritual quality. All religions have made it difficult to laugh. The sense of humour has not been recognised by any religion as a religious quality. I declare it to be the highest religious quality and if we can decide that every year, for one hour, at a certain date, a certain time, the whole world will laugh, I think it will help to dispel darkness and violence because laughter is the only human characteristic which no animal possesses.

"All animals are incapable of laughter, and whenever these religions make somebody a saint, he becomes like an animal for he loses laughter. He falls down the evolutionary ladder, not rising any higher.

"Laughter has a beauty, a multidimensional one. It can relax you; it can suddenly make you feel light; it can make your world devoid of burden, but a beautiful experience [sic]. It can change everything in your life. Just the touch of laughter can make life worth living, something to be grateful for."

Passive Listening

Morning is the best time to energise yourself. It is the best time for meditation. It is the time when the whole existence is waking up and one can try different meditative methods.

The moment you wake up, get connected with your being. And the best way to get connected is to become aware of your breath. Watch your breath coming in, going out. Watch it. Don't breathe, just watch. Watch passively. Listen to the soft and subtle sound of the movement of your breath. Listen to the birds chirping outside your house. The sound of utensils in the kitchen. The milkman has come and he is talking to your mother. The newspaper boy has dropped the paper outside your door. You can hear the sound of vehicles on the roads. These are situations over which you have no control. You can listen passively and there is no need to get involved or to judge them. Just listen to them in their totality without choosing anything.

This can be the best method of relaxation and acceptance. Later in the day you can stand somewhere on the footpath and watch the traffic go by. You have nothing to do with the traffic. So many things are happening and you are not involved. You are simply watching.

Now doing the same passive listening in the morning

when in bed is a good start of the day to experience relaxation. You develop patience and slowly and consciously become free from any kind of rashness or roughness in your behaviour. Listen passively in all its totality — the sounds coming from the kitchen and street; the aroma of food being cooked, everything is reaching your senses. This is something that you have not created, yet it is there. You can just accept it without any involvement.

Now move the arrow of your consciousness within. There is a traffic of all kinds of thoughts. They are there. You have not invited them. They are not your conscious creation. As you watch the traffic on the road by standing aloof, watch these thoughts too, but don't get involved. Your mind is broadcasting thoughts. You can hear them; they are so loud that they have their own sounds and visuals. Just watch and listen to the talk going on inside your head and look for the gaps. You will notice the small gaps in between. Be alert and stay in the gap; it may not happen on the first day. It might take several days to find gaps. But there's nothing to worry about and no need to get impatient. Just enjoy this passive listening and watching and stay in your being.

Now, after this you can get up and walk to your bathroom. Remember to remain inside your body with full awareness when you get out. Stay tuned as you walk. In the shower, let every cell of your being feel the wonderful sensation of water. Be a child, play with water, but always remain alert inside. Let the water drop alternately on different parts of your body and feel life arising in those parts. Finally let there be a feeling of liveliness in your whole body.

This liveliness is divine. Remember to enjoy this whole thing. Be playful. Being playful is the real knack of meditation.

A Journey Within

It's morning now. You are waking up. Become aware that you are waking up. There's no need to hurry. Before getting out of bed, just connect with yourself, your being. Feel yourself. Feel that you are waking up. Feel yourself. Feel the blessing of the coming of awakening, as a lotus opens its petals and sways in the fresh, cool morning breeze.

Before getting out of bed, enter your body consciously. Take your consciousness everywhere in your body. Start with the feet. Move your consciousness to your left foot. Be there for a while. Feel it. Now move your attention to your right foot. Be there for a while. Feel it. Repeat this process of moving your consciousness towards your feet alternately. Giving attention is like imparting energy, making your feet come alive. They deserve your love. They will carry you around the whole day, whole life. Just recognise them.

Move your consciousness upwards within your body. Bring your attention to your navel centre. Stay there for a while. Check your breathing. Watch your breath come in and go out. Be one with your breath. Feel that you are the breath. Riding on the breath, remain passive and attentive.

Now move your consciousness to your heart. Feel the sweetness of your heart. Feel the goodness, the sensitivity of your heart. This is the very nature of your heart. Feel that you are love, only love and nothing else.

Now let your attention move to your throat. Stay inside your throat. You use this instrument excessively the whole day. Now is the time to give some energy to it. From the throat, enter your face. This is something that you show to the world the whole day. Being inside your face with full consciousness will make your face glow brighter.

Feel your chin from within, your lips, your nose, your ears and eyes. Keep your eyes closed and feel them from within. About 80 per cent of the energy spent by our eyes is on looking outside during the day. Give the energy back to your eyes. Attention to the eyes from within will naturally take your energy to the middle of your eyes — your third eye centre. Here you can stay a little longer. This centre is your bridge to the beyond.

Now take your energy all over your head. Feel your head from within. Your head is tired and exhausted because of the constant traffic of thoughts and worries — mostly useless and meaningless. Feeling this centre with all your energy will make it healthy and function better. If the mind is healthy and sound, there can be no problem in the world.

Now is the time to move away from your head, go to your shoulders and enter your arms — to the left arm and then to the right arm. Let your energy reach your hands; let them become warm. Feel the warmth in your hands. Rub the hands gently and place them on your face. Shower this energy on your face, specially on your eyes. Now your whole being is full of energy; you are ready to start the day, energetically and enthusiastically. Energy is a delight. Feel delighted.

Do this experiment in your bed for a few days. We will employ some other methods a few days later. Remember one thing — be sincere in your meditation, but there's no need of any seriousness. It's a journey of bliss.

Bring God Within You

You have heard that God is everywhere, in everything, in every leaf of the tree, in stars and even in dust particles. But if I declare that you are also God, you may not believe me. You will probably say, "Me? God? I am such an angry, greedy man, how can I be God?" But the alchemy is that the moment you accept that you are God, you will not be an angry or greedy man.

Our mind accepts divinity, godliness, in everything except in our own selves. Dust particles may have godliness but not us! I suggest a meditation — this new gestalt of accepting godliness within yourself and the moment you start accepting this, you will not remain the same person again. There will be a mutation in your consciousness, an inner revolution. So tonight when you go to bed, God is going to sleep within you. Feel it. It does not matter what you have been doing the whole day. Forget it. Remember only one thing — God is going to sleep. This feeling will change the quality of your sleep. Your sleep will continue with this quality through the night and you will wake up with the same feeling.

You will wake up with the feeling that God is also awake. If it doesn't happen, do it consciously. Remain in bed for a while and feel that God is waking up. Feel in every cell of your being that God is awakening within you. There is nothing else but God. Godliness is just another name of consciousness. Consciousness is the stuff we are all made of. We are not matter, we are not mind — we are consciousness. The moment we start realising this, we start glowing with consciousness. This glorious consciousness knows no misery, no anguish. It is made of bliss. It is truth. *Sat chit anand.*

If you have a taste of godliness within your being, even though it may be very tiny, it will lead you to truth, consciousness and bliss. If you start your day with such a remembrance, it will grow daily and your taste will become permanent. You will breathe godliness.

Remember, there is no need to become greedy about godliness. Start with this small experience within yourself and let it expand naturally. The moment will come one day when you will feel yourself full of godliness. In such moments, the enlightened ones declare: *Aham Brahmasmi* (I am God). Let godliness pervade your being. Feel your consciousness spreading into every nook and corner of your being. Let your whole being become illuminated. Then everything that exists within you and without, is nothing but godliness.

You walk in God, you talk in God. The mystic Kabir sings:

Uthoon baithoon so parikrama.

(No matter what you do, sit or stand, it is nothing else but being in meditation.)

Now through you God feels and God thinks. It's all God's play. It is his *lila*. Celebrate this moment.

In the Meadow of Meditation

Meditation is knowing oneself, feeling at par with the self, experiencing the inner self from its very core. In the last 'wake up' morning meditation, we glimpsed the art of touching and tasting our own being from within. Now we take a step further; walk on. How do you feel? Do you feel very alive? Would you like to go deeper within yourself? Do you want to turn this glimpse into a permanent looking glass?

If you think so, please give up the idea. It is not possible. Nothing is permanent; change is bound to take place. Remember, not to get stuck with any single experience. Learn to move on.

Any experience, howsoever delightful it may be, can create bondage if we don't leave it and move ahead. Any experience, if not moved away from after its time has lapsed, can put fetters on you. And meditation is freedom — freedom unlimited; in fact it is freedom from experience itself. In the beginning you will go through all kinds of experiences — experiences that may tempt you to cling on to them.

If you falter and linger on, you become incapable of climbing higher or delving deep into unknown territories. And as the mystics say, the ultimate is unknown. It is a supreme mystery. So let's see what can be done as an effective morning meditation, which will bring about a qualitative change in our daily lives.

Laughter is a powerful meditation method suggested by mystics and scientists as it provides a central meeting point for science and spirituality. Laughing is the best remedy to improve your health and your life. Laughter is said to be even healthier than jogging. Scientists have shown that an optimistic attitude towards life helps regulate hormones, which in turn strengthen the immune system. Those who laugh whole-heartedly are physically more active and less prone to bad habits.

And remember, there is a lot of difference between soulful laughter and laughing at a person. We are talking about pure, soulful laughter; the one which does not hurt anybody. This pure laughter can be transformed into a meditation. Only such laughter can penetrate every fibre of your being and nourish it from within. Your being will emanate with laughter which will dispel the gloom and have a soothing effect on others.

So, when you wake up in the morning, the first thing to do is to start laughing consciously. Though you as well as others may not think very highly of your mental sanity, do not allow these perceived notions of madness to impede laughter. These socially-accepted perceptions of madness are in fact much worse than your so-called madness. But this madness proves better than your so-called sanity; it leads to real sanity and health.

Start laughing consciously. Put in as much energy as possible into the laughter exercise. Soon you will see that your laughter becomes natural. When the laughter subsides, close your eyes and enter your being. Feel the liveliness generated by your laughter. Fall deep into your silence. Laughter leading to silence is the taste of meditation. This is the real tonic for your health and happiness.

Understanding Meditation

People often complain, "I don't have time for meditation." It is true that they don't have time for something that will not give them money. There are others who complain that they have so much time that they don't know what to do with it.

They have no money problem; the only problem is time. So much time! They watch television, read newspapers, go to clubs and the race-course or they play cards or chess. But in spite of all these occupations, they feel bored.

Time or no time is not the real issue. The issue is to understand whether we really need time for meditation or not. For a man of understanding, meditation is a lifestyle, not separate from life. It is the way of living or one can call it the art of living.

Or if you are of a scientific temperament, you can call it the science of living. There is another appropriate word: *knack*. Yes, meditation is a sort of knack.

You can call it in modern psychological terms: gestalt. Change your gestalt and you can be in meditation.

Meditation is just like breathing; you don't need any separate time to breathe, otherwise, you will die, if, for a single moment you forget to breathe. You are walking, you are sitting — all the activities are going on and you are breathing as well. You don't need a separate time to breathe. You don't tell your wife or friend, "Hang on, let me have a break and go out to breathe." That would sound ridiculous. You know that breathing is going on without your being aware about it.

Meditation can be as natural as breathing. It can go on all through the day, non-stop. Meditation is nothing but awareness, a witnessing of consciousness. Bring awareness to everything you do — walking, talking, eating, sitting and sleeping. Let the arrow of your awareness come towards you. You stand in a crowded bus, lost in your thoughts about what you will do when you reach home. And there are others in the bus with similar thoughts. And they step on each other's toes and get into unnecessary fights. It is because nobody is really where he should be.

This is what happens on a wider scale too. The river of life keeps flowing without our awareness. Lack of awareness is the real cause of all our miseries. The man of meditation will change all this. He will first become aware of his unawareness. He will witness that he is acting mechanically. He will start becoming aware in all his acts — big or small. Many things that bring misery in life because of lack of awareness will automatically disappear.

We always do things in unawareness and repent later — I should not have done this, I should not have said that. But repentance or feeling sorry doesn't solve anything. It works almost like a chain — we act unconsciously and out of habit, we repent. This is a vicious circle, which creates bondage.

The fire of awareness burns all this bondage and sets us free from the chain reaction. Mediation is freedom; freedom to act consciously. Consciousness knows no misery. It is joy. I will discuss more about how we can be in a state of constant meditation in my later pieces.

Preparation for *Vipassana*

Today the most commonly known method of meditation is *vipassana*. Recently, the Delhi police were on the front pages of Delhi newspapers, doing this meditation. From the murderers in Tihar Jail to supercop Kiran Bedi and supermodels like Madhu Sapre have done *vipassana*. Members of Parliament also learnt it recently.

The word *vipassana* seems to have become synonymous with meditation. In fact, it is. It is very simple but our life is such that all simple things become complicated because we have become complicated ourselves. So simple things look very tough. Otherwise, just sitting and watching the breath go in and come out is the simplest thing one can do. But do that for yourself and see — you will come to know how difficult it is.

You will think about all kinds of nonsensical and useless things, except for watching your breath. You will become bored within five minutes and get up and start doing something else. You can only sit for a longer time and watch your breath if you first become physically tired and exhausted.

In earlier days, when there was lots to do physically and life was simple, *vipassana* could be done very easily. A woodcutter chops wood in the forest and when he is tired, he sits down and watches his breath. His relaxation is as deep as meditation. His sleep is the deepest. The modern man knows nothing of deep mediation or deep sleep, which in *yogic* terms is called *sushupti*. So, *vipassana* is very effective but the context is missing. One needs a little activity before entering into *vipassana* — a bit of jogging or a morning walk, or some fast and chaotic breathing. Then find a good spot where you can sit down and watch your breath. While you inhale, your attention should go in with the air. Be alert and aware when your breath takes a turn. Stay there. When you breathe out, let your attention move with it. This practice will provide you with such a knack that it will become natural and effortless.

In Tao wisdom, effort is the door to effortlessness. All effort is a preparation for meditation. *Yogic* postures are not meditation; they are merely a preparation. So don't be tempted to go into *vipassana* straight away, without preparation. Otherwise you will become dull and dead. There are many people who meditate but look utterly dull and lifeless, without any glow on their face.

Meditation is something alive and sparkling. It will bring a glow to your face. If it doesn't happen, then your meditation is not right; it is not working. Meditation works certainly, and works wonders, only when you prepare for it without any hurry and greed.

Meditation should make you more sensitive and sensuous – overflowing with life. Your presence exudes such life, such energy that heals and cheers up others around you.

Shake your being thoroughly. It doesn't matter how you do it. Enter *vipassana.* Fill yourself first with fresh life-energy that surrounds you. Only then are you ready to glide naturally into the deep valley of this meditation.

Recharging Yourself

A few moments of meditation is all it takes to energise the tired body and mind.

Meditation has caught on like wild fire — from Pune to Pennsylvania and from Mumbai to Manhattan. It's found its way into the mainstream media too — be it in print or on the Net. For physical ailments too, meditation is proving to be a part of the treatment process. If you have heart problems, check with your regular doctor. But also consult a meditation teacher, as that can lighten your heart.

In fact, government hospitals and state universities are giving high priority to research in meditation. The East has known the magic of meditation all along and has been practicing it. But somewhere along the line, it seems to have forgotten it. It is now finding its way back, but on recommendation from the West. Especially the urban class that is very much in step with the West these days.

For example, we have known it in the East that if you have a headache, go out and breathe for a few moments. Inhale from the left nostril seven times and exhale from the left, and repeat it in the reverse order. There will be an automatic balance in *yin* and *yang* energy and the headache will disappear in no time. There will be no need for painkillers, which have so many side effects and are addictive too.

Meditation is simple. But our life has become so complex that simple things don't attract us any more. There lies the whole problem. Let's take an example from our daily life. When we try to log on to our computers and don't get the connection, we really become irritated at the long wait. We want to see our important messages but getting a connection takes a long time, so we don't know what to do.

MEDITATE!

Close your eyes. Breathe. Watch your breath going in. Go as deep with it as possible and see where it takes a turn before coming back with it. Do it in the gaps when you are waiting for your mail to be downloaded! Breathing will energise your whole system and closing your eyes for a few moments will refresh them.

There's a very big computer company in Europe, Sidoun, which has its headquarters at Freiburg, Germany. The staff does gibberish meditation before getting down to their routine. In those few moments they throw out all the garbage accumulated in the basket of the subconscious mind. It becomes easier for them to start afresh. They feel happy and light and get prepared to tackle another day's work.

Balancing *Vipassana*

If done right, *vipassana* can reap immense benefits for you as it is a very powerful form of meditation. The best time to do it is early morning or any time before lunch, i.e. if you are in the habit of waking up late.

In the beginning, an hour of meditation is more than enough. Don't rush into 10-day-long meditation camps where you have to sit for hours at a stretch daily. Anything excessive in the beginning may prove very harmful. Many people make the mistake of over-indulgence in *vipassana.*

One has to guard against this spiritual greed. It is the same greedy mind, which earlier ran after money, sex and power, but now it is doing *shirshasana* and running after a spiritual experience.

Our body goes through an unhealthy shock if it is subjected to sudden changes. Meditation needs proper preparation, thus our body has to be treated like a temple of the divine, and not be forced into any unnatural lifestyle. The other thing one needs to remember is that if you do *vipassana* for an hour, find time to do some dancing meditation to balance it. If you only do *vipassana,* you may become serious, stiff and stony. Practice of *vipassana* might make the body rigid. It is not supposed to be that way. The more flexible and light the body is, the more beautiful and relaxing is the experience. So find time to dance or do some aerobics. That would strike a healthy balance. You can do it the other way round too: First dance and then do *vipassana.*

It all depends on what the needs of your body are and how your body reacts to new situations. Remember one thing — do not be unnatural and don't force your body too much. The body has its own limitations; try to discover that. It is wiser than the mind. So listen to it and have reverence for it. It is your body, which is a means to realise the ultimate truth. The third point to remember is not to do *vipassana* in the evening or before going to sleep. This may disrupt your sleep as exercise at night can generate so much energy that you won't know what to do with this energy. Your body needs rest at night and any meditation that creates a lot of energy at night can affect your sleep. It may lead to irritation, which may continue till the next day.

Vipassana should remain healthy meditation and not become an unhealthy irritation. So the best time to do this meditation is certainly the morning time when the air is fresh and the whole of existence is waking up. The sun is rising and the birds are singing. This collective awakening helps in the awakening of the individual. It becomes easier to feel one with universal consciousness.

Discovering the Zing in Living!

There's more to life than just living, and meditation can help you find that deeper meaning.

Once a disciple asked his master, "Why is there so much misery in the world?"

The master replied, "There's so much misery because you don't practice meditation. Meditation is not a priority in your life; it's like the last item on your laundry list. The day you make it your priority, there won't be any misery."

The master continued, "Please don't talk about the misery in the world; nothing can be done about that. There's misery in the life of an individual, and that can be dealt with directly. The individual can transform himself. Once that happens, the world will get transformed automatically, as the world consists of only individuals. There's no jungle; there are only individual trees."

The disciple had asked about the world and the master turned it around and changed the focus. He created an urgency in the mind of the disciple by emphasising: "Don't worry about the world. Pay attention to yourself. Go out and see! The birds are singing. There's a continuous celebration in Nature. Why is man so miserable and out of sync with existence?"

Man has forgotten how to live. There's no celebration in

his life because there is no meditation. Yes, there is an endless amount of entertainment, but that is not celebration. This overdose of entertainment does not end his misery. Meditation is the real cure to put an end to misery. This is the only cure that works — and works wonders. So the first thing to do is to bring meditation on the top of your list. Don't start your day without meditation. And the first and foremost meditation I suggest is that when you are awake, start laughing and do it loudly. Don't be miserly in laughter, but have a hearty laugh. Include your family too in it!

Life is so hilariously ridiculous that there can be no response other than laughter. Do it before you read your daily newspapers. Then even when you read the news, you will continue laughing. When you read, "Rabri gets bail and Laloo gets jail", you can laugh. There is so much poetry in life and yet you don't laugh. Don't become too serious about it. Laughter is more meaningful than all our serious intellectual discussions. They have destroyed millions of trees to feed you daily with such ridiculously unhealthy news. And the news brings nothing but misery. I suggest that you go out of your house and find a spot in Nature. Go ahead and hug a tree. Time may come when it will become difficult to find a tree in your neighbourhood. Hug the tree deeply for a few moments and it will fill you with lots of life-energy. You will feel uplifted and relieved. Find some moments early in the morning to meditate under a tree. Fill your lungs with oxygen to make an energetic start of your day. You would create your own energy field under the tree if you sit in meditation daily. There will not be any misery in your life, as you will have more life force in your life. You don't have to be a beggar when you can have so much life-energy around you. You can be the emperor of your inner world.

Flight of the Alone

Being alone with yourself and understanding yourself is the way to peace.

Man, as he is and as he lives, is a crowd. He appears to be a single unit, but in reality, a crowd of people lives in him — all his relationships exist in him at the same time. So when he enters within himself, many images of his relationships come floating to him. At no time is he able to feel himself in entirety, in purity — just himself and nothing else. This situation continues through his whole life; even in the next life.

You may have heard that some people are born with all the memories of their previous life. Everybody carries with him his load of memories and images — that's what makes him a crowd. Entering into meditation becomes difficult, almost impossible, because of all this stuff. It is a real *sadhana* to go beyond this, or bypass this load. We have carried this burden and we have become one with it. How to disentangle ourselves from this mess is the whole science of meditation.

There are many methods but what is needed first is the understanding of our situation — not intellectually, but actually. One has to sit alone and find some minutes or hours of solitude to come face to face with one's true self. That needs courage. People have the courage to go out and meet people, but rarely do they have the courage to meet themselves. They run away from any situation that entails being alone. If in the beginning one can manage a few hours of aloneness, one can get ready for a 21-day period of isolation. For creating intensity in meditation and transformation, the period of 21 days can be really helpful. Much is possible in this period.

To begin with, one has to be courageous to go into this period of being alone. Nobody else can do it for you. This journey is basically a flight of the alone to the alone. Aloneness is our permanent reality; other things come and go; even relationships come and go. They will affect you, bind you, possess you but they can never become you. In your deepest core you will remain utterly alone. Even your so-called deepest love affairs fade away in course of time. They may leave indelible impressions or scar your psyche, but they don't become you — they remain only a burden or bundle of memories.

Courage is needed to free oneself from all this and see oneself in purity. This is real liberation. Remember the words of Gautama the Buddha: "Therefore, Ananda, be ye lamps unto yourselves, be ye a refuge to yourselves. Betake yourselves to no external refuge. Hold fast to the truth as a lamp; hold fast to the truth as a refuge. Look not for a refuge in anyone besides yourselves."

The Eastern Lesson

A holistic approach in medicine is what we must all imbibe.

In ancient India, we looked at the human being as an organic whole — of the body, mind and sprit. When I say 'ancient', I do not mean thousands of years ago. I use the word as an indication of a way of life, not in the sense of a time period. Even now, there are some regions in the country where Western civilisation has not influenced local life.

With Western civilisation came the craze for specialisation and with specialisation came division. So now we have doctors for all parts of the body, but who know nothing about the body, mind or soul. We have psychiatrists who don't know anything about physical health; and about the soul, they are utterly confused. Specialisation does have a very significant role to play in the health care of humans, but it can prove very harmful if it does not take into account the other aspects too. Treating the body without knowing the effects on the mind and soul is like treating the leaves and forgetting the hidden roots.

Man is a psychosomatic being. Western medicine has been operating under the fallacious assumption that the mind and body are separate entities and that they should be treated separately because they have nothing to do with each other.

But of late, some research done in the West has contradicted this assumption. They have realised that treating the entire person – in body, mind and spirit – can yield more beneficial medical results.

Earlier, Western cardiologists focused on the heart and did not seek a body-mind-spirit approach to treating and preventing heart conditions. Their method was to treat existing problems with surgery or medication. Dr Erminia Guarneri, Medical Director of the Scripps Ornish Program at the Scripps Foundation for Medicine and Science, believes that this hasty approach is an aspect of Western medicine that must change.

"We have to look beyond physical healing," Guarneri asserts. "We have to take a look at the whole person because the mental, emotional and even the spiritual aspects of healing cannot be separated from the physical."

Dr Naresh Trehan, the famous cardiologist, is of a similar opinion when he says that meditation and alternative therapy play a very significant role in treating heart disease. He says he has learned some meditation techniques and these could be very useful in controlling stress, which is the major cause of heart attacks.

A study conducted by the medical school at Harvard University indicated through its findings that patients who have suffered from one heart attack can reduce the risk of a second attack if they learn to stay calm during emotional conflicts. Similar studies by the Mayo Clinic concluded that psychological stress is the strongest indicator of possible cardiac conditions.

Meditation teaches us the knack of remaining calm and composed in all emotionally charged and other stressful situations. Stress aggravates high blood pressure, diabetes and heart disease. It is important to find ways to deal with stress in the initial stage with meditation and thereby prevent later health problems. A 20-year study of 730 heart patients revealed that those suffering from depression were 70 per cent more likely to have a heart attack than those who were not.

This research supports the ancient Eastern approach that advocates a connection between body, mind and spirit.

Universal Intelligence

"It has changed my life. It has changed my relationships. It has transformed my sex life too" — this is what people in the West say about meditation. They want their life to be happy, to work out fine, and for that they seek refuge in mediation. Meditation is the modern *mantra* for the new generation.

The old generation has been living with its own belief systems and fighting about them endlessly. The new generation sees the futility of these conflicting ideologies and is going for the real science of transformation.

Yes, meditation is nothing else but the science of transformation. It eliminates conflict and equips you with the tools of transformation, so that you can live your life with happiness and enthusiasm, with energy and ecstasy. Meditation has become a must for the health-conscious new generation. "I never leave the house without meditating," is what they say. In fact, morning is the best time for meditation. It can be called the breakfast for the soul. Meditation is not concentration as is commonly perceived both in the East and West. It is the wholeness of your body, mind and soul.

Showering just before meditating is good because it refreshes your whole being, and makes it easier for the effects of meditation to reach every fibre of your body. You can go to the roof of your house or find a spot in your garden to meditate. Let the rising sun and the cool breeze touch you. Exhale the impurities and toxins out of your system and inhale the purity of the morning. Do it deeply and energetically. Don't worry about the duration. Do it as long as it feels natural, as it is only the quality that matters, not the quantity.

Remember only one word about meditation — be natural. Any unnatural force will create unnecessary conflicts in your already burdened life. Discard everything that is not natural in your life and you will be happy. Be at ease. Ease is what is necessary. Close your eyes for a few minutes and feel oneness with the existence that surrounds you — the sunlight, the cool breeze and the sound of birds!

After this breakfast for the soul, you will relish not just your regular breakfast but all your daily activities. You will usher in the same unhurried quality of meditation into every aspect of your life. Your communication and dealing with work-mates will be coloured in shades of vibrancy. A mutual sense of respect will grow. The relationship will not be hampered by competition but enhanced by cooperation. You will be motivated towards excellence and creativity and not feel like pursuing the single-minded motive of success at any cost.

A life that believes in sharing is the life of bliss. Pursuit of private goals creates much misery as it uses others for personal ambitions. Heraclitus even warns us about our private intelligence and tells us to become one with the universal intelligence.

It can Perform Magic!

People often inquire, "Which is the right place to meditate?" It is a very significant question. If we find a particular place where we feel good and it offers a good ambience, then that's the place. We should meditate daily at that particular place. By our daily meditation, the place acquires a certain character, an energy-field, which becomes conducive to meditation.

The place then welcomes you the moment you return there to meditate. This whole existence is about life. The trees and earth and sky are all life. When we meditate at a certain place, the place turns more lively by our regular meditation. It contains our energy, the energy of meditation, and inherits the vibrations from our calmness and silence. And each time that we meditate there, the preserved energy becomes available to us. It becomes a common heartbeat between the person and the place where the meditation occurs.

It happened once that a man came to see a Zen master. The man was not very sensitive. When he entered the meditation room of the master, he closed the door loudly with a bang. The Zen master told the man: "First go back to the door and seek its forgiveness. You have been very insensitive with the door."

The man understood the point and went back to the door to ask for forgiveness. Thus the Zen master gave him the first very important lesson of meditation: treat everything with sensitivity — even those things which do not look alive. There is life everywhere. Before you enter the field of meditation, become alert and aware. Bring in the quality of sensitivity with you. Meditation is going to make you more sensitive and intuitive. You will become more alive — full of abundance and with a sense of life you have never known before. You will feel a general feeling of friendliness toward all. This existence will stop seeming inimical and hostile. You will carry that aura of friendliness and calmness that meditation brings. This will touch others too, but most importantly, it will enhance that place where you meditate. It will actually welcome you.

The temples too breathe such life. Just by bowing your head mechanically at these places of worship you cannot make them into a temple. Only if someone meditates at some place sincerely does that place become a temple.

Gautama the Buddha meditated under a Bodhi tree and one day there was an explosion of enlightenment. The blessed Bodhi tree was a witness to this ultimate explosion and imbibed the vibrations. The tree remains alive even today. It has become a unique temple and a symbol of inspiration to thousands of seekers. Such is the magic of meditation.

Dreaming and Meditation

Meditation seeks to concentrate on the dreamer rather than the dreams. We are all dreamers. Dreaming is our reality. During the day most of our energy remains involved in thinking. During the night, in our sleep, the same energy moves towards dreams.

Our dreams create such images that these seem more real than reality! And we connect with that reality during the sleeping hours. We dream that somebody has killed us, and we wake up trembling and crying. We fancy a woman during the day — some beauty queen or a film star — and we don't get her. This creates starvation and deprivation. We sleep with these images floating in our dreams during our sleep. And dreams are very compassionate. They give us what we yearn for.

But next morning begins a day of harsh reality and frustration. This is the story of everybody who is a normal person. There are people who can be called below normal. They think that the dreams they see during the night are for real and that they have to be pursued until made real. Normal people are amazed at their dreams and forget them in moments to continue with their daily routine. Above-normal people meditate over their dreams and go in the direction of self-realisation.

One famous Taoist master, Chuang Tsu, who is known in the world for his unique and incomparable stories, got up one morning feeling very sad. He sat in his bed and called his disciples. They came to him and inquired: "Master, what has happened? We have never seen you so sad in your whole life. What is the problem?"

Chuang Tsu replied, "You will not understand my problem. This is really a difficult problem. I don't think you can solve this one. Even I cannot solve this."

The disciples insisted. Chuang Tsu said, "Well, then. Try to solve it. Last night I saw a dream. In the dream I became a butterfly!"

The disciples said, "It is not a problem. Dreams are dreams. Just forget them."

The master replied, "No, you don't understand. The problem is bigger and more complex. Now what is troubling me is that I am thinking about a possibility. Last night in the dream Chuang Tsu became a butterfly. So it creates another possibility that now the same butterfly may be dreaming of becoming a Chuang Tsu. Who is real — the butterfly or Chuant Tsu? Can anybody solve this problem? Who am I — Chuang Tsu or the butterfly?"

Dreams are dreams. Meditation is not concerned with dreams. It is concerned with the reality behind the dreams — about the one who is dreaming. The arrow has to go in that direction. Attention needs to be directed towards the dreamer, who has to turn in towards himself or herself. Tonight when you go to sleep, suggest to your mind that as soon as you start dreaming, you will become aware and focus your energy away from the eyes and on your third eye — the centre between the two eyes. You will realise your witnessing self and dreams will disappear. The eyes see outside; dreams also come to you from outside. The third eye sees itself in your inside, your inner self. This is meditation.

Be a Light Unto Yourself

"*Sammasati*! Remember that you are a Buddha!" These last words are said to have been uttered by Gautama the Buddha. For a Buddha, this whole world becomes a Buddha as he sees the world in his own light.

For a man of illumination, the same light is seen in every being. There is no distinction or discrimination between big and small, holy or unholy. Such a thing does not exist in the vision of an enlightened person. The only difference that is seen is that someone is sleeping and someone has been awakened.

The awakened ones don't make this big issue. They are compassionate to all those who are not yet awakened and share their light with them without any judgement or condemnation. They are unable to reject or condemn anybody. Even a person like Angulimal receives Buddha's compassion as much as any other *bhikshu*. Putting his own life into grave danger, Gautama the Buddha goes to him also and finally transforms him into a *bhikshu*. In the encounter, compassion wins and violence surrenders. Such is the power of sharing illumination without discrimination. Who can transform a criminal like Angulimal, who is ready to kill even his own mother?

Only a person like Buddha who has no fear of being

killed and has absolute trust that the Divine resides in the criminal also. He believes that one has only to invoke it by sharing one's light. It is said that "thousands of candles can be lit from a single candle, and the life of the candle will not be shortened. Happiness never decreases by sharing."

There are many priests who want to be addressed as His Holiness or things like that. But in the eyes of Buddha, there's no such thing as holy or unholy; people are either awakened or not awakened. Awakening comes with meditation.

That's the case with all the sleeping Buddhas. When one person realises his enlightenment, he starts reminding other sleeping Buddhas to wake up. Like the famous Indian mystic Kabir sings: "*Sadho, jaagat neend na keeje*!" Kabir also addresses them as *Sadho,* even though they are asleep.

Alan Cohen says, "I met a man who called everyone he met the 'Buddha'. 'How are you doing today, Buddha?' he would ask me. 'Beautiful sunset, don't you think, Buddha?' At first I felt jarred by his magnanimous appellation. Then I began to really like it. It felt better than 'Dude'."

Once a *bhikshu* asked Buddha, "Are you the messiah?"

"No," answered the Buddha.

"Then are you a teacher?" the *bhikshu* persisted.

"No, I am not a teacher."

"Then what are you?" asked the *bhikshu*.

"I am awake," Buddha replied.

Buddha simply means awakening, illumination and enlightenment. And everybody who wants enlightenment has to go on the path of meditation. Meditation leads to compassion. One doesn't have to cultivate compassion; it comes as a by-product of meditation. One has to put in every effort to light his lamp. Another most significant statement of Gautama the Buddha is: "Be a light unto yourself."

Meditation is the art and science of lighting one's

own lamp. Meditation does not require any priest. It cuts the very roots of priesthood. It is an independent journey of oneself, leading to ultimate awakening. We have to trust our small lamp within us and carry on our meditation.

Staying in Tune

A method of meditation which has been effective in the last 10,000 years includes watching one's breath. This method has never failed simply because it brings our whole consciousness in the moment. Meditation also means the art of being in the moment — no past, no future; just in this moment.

When we pray or chant a *mantra,* our mind can wander in all directions. Thinking continues. Calculations go on. The mind becomes full of market — a *la juna* bazaar. We may start dreaming or having an inner dialogue with our beloved or wife, friend or an enemy. It does not matter with whom — we may start talking with the Almighty God of our own imagination. We may create a hallucination. Everything that our mind does, takes us to the past or the future. And what brings us back in the moment? The breathing.

We cannot breathe in the past or the future. It is simply impossible. When we breathe, our thinking also stops because breathing needs all the attention.

You cannot divide the attention. Breath generates a certain amount of energy in the body that has its own effect. In certain meditation methods, vigorous breathing takes place. Such methods are even better than simple methods of watching the breath. Such methods bring deeper relaxation and when you relax later, you can watch your breath passively and naturally and continue to remain in the moment.

In *vipassana* one goes inward with the breath consciously and comes out with it consciously. There's no time gap in between. You are not thinking of exhaling when you are inhaling. You are not thinking of inhaling when you are exhaling. Try this method and see what happens to you in this process. Go on to the terrace or some other solitary place where there's no possibility of any interference. For some time, as long as you feel, breathe vigorously — bring all your energy to exhaling and inhaling. The moment will come naturally when you will feel like sitting down or just standing or you may even want to lie down. Do that.

Then watch your breath going in and coming out. You will feel the deepest rest and total relaxation, besides getting a glimpse of meditation. With such techniques you can always find your own rhythm and time limit. Meditation is not an action. It actually happens when all action stops and the mind stops. It is an intense feeling of unknown energy that resides within us. This energy is really a delight and celebration.

If you start your day like this, you become enlightened. An early dose of this energy will work wonders for the rest of the day. You will move with a confidence you have never known before. When your work-mates start noticing this change, you can invite them to join you. Then even your office can become tension-free and a place of meditation.

Meditation shared on a large scale can bring about a revolution, which our dull offices need so urgently. Come on, breathe some energy into your office. You have nothing to lose but some dullness!

Breathe Your Anger Away

The other day there was a report on a study that stated that anger and hostility as character traits may start damaging the arteries of even young adults. A 10-year study of 374 black and white adults between the ages of 18 to 30 found that those who displayed high levels of anger and hostility were more likely to develop artery calcification. This may not produce recognisable symptoms, but can lead to heart disease.

One need not be a scientist or researcher to know the effects of anger on one's health. One only needs to be sensitive. The being of an angry person transmits vibrations of anger and violence around. Just standing close to such a person may make you feel nauseated. His very presence can be uncomfortable. On the other hand, when you stand close to one who meditates, you will feel uplifted; a kind of comfortable feeling will surround you. If vibrations can affect another person, then imagine how much more they would affect the person who is always carrying them, living with them? It must be hell for him.

A simple tree comes to know immediately when a woodcutter draws close to it with the intention of cutting it down. Scientists have measured the fear of such a tree. And they are able to measure the happiness and joy of plants when a gardener comes to take care of them. They understand such vibrations — both positive and negative. But man is becoming more and more insensitive to such vibrations. He remains so lost in his own thoughts that he cannot feel the vibrations around him. Otherwise it would have been possible for him to be free from such unhealthy situations, which abound in anger and violence.

It is not merely the arteries that are getting blocked or clogged, but the very consciousness that is shrinking. And that is worse than physical poison. That is actually a retardation of sorts; a mental block.

What is the answer to such a malady?

Meditation is the answer.

Meditation makes us sensitive human beings. It helps us to detox ourselves by getting rid of the foreign elements in our system. There are cathartic methods and gibberish, which are very effective. These methods can easily be done in the privacy of the bathroom because we cannot openly demonstrate our cumulative madness. At the same time, we cannot preserve or suppress this poison within us for a longer period as it may erupt like a volcano one day.

So the best way out is to do a daily cleaning during some moments of catharsis and gibberish to rid ourselves of our inner garbage. It will make us lighter and healthier, making us at the same time friendlier to those around us. Our vibrations will convey the message of love, friendship and sensitive people will certainly receive it.

There's a beautiful quote in the *Atharva Veda*:

"Cast off anger from your heart, like an arrow from the bow, so that you may again be friends and live together in harmony."

A New Chain of Smoke

Every year on May 31, the United Nations observes 'No Tobacco Day' Such anti-this and anti-that days are observed without fail, all over the world. One day the newspapers reported that the tobacco toll since 1 January 2000 has been more than 1.5 million. It is reported that tobacco kills 11,000 people each day. On May 31, more than 1.60 million people would have been killed by tobacco only. And here we thought AIDS was the greatest killer!

Scientific researchers say that smokers are low on heart protection. Compared with non-smokers, smokers have lower levels of para oxnase (PON), a protein in the blood that provides protection against coronary artery disease. They found that coronary artery disease was more likely to be absent among non-smokers (absent in 29.7 per cent) than among current smokers (19.7 per cent) and ex-smokers (15.0 per cent). The more we read such scientific research, the more depressed we get. But convey these reports to smokers and they will laugh them away in smoke.

They simply do not care. They say. "So what if we live a few years less than non-smokers? At least we enjoy our life. What do you gain by living longer than us?"

They do have their own logic, and sometimes that can make more sense than that of non-smokers!

Smokers are generally a stubborn lot of helpless people. By reminding them about their habit again and again and by preaching to them constantly, we end up making them feel guilty and self-pitiable. Put on the defensive, they become even more stubborn — they smoke more and cause more self-destruction. Further, out of sheer helplessness and frustration at not being able to stop or control this habit, they say, "What can we do? How can we get rid of this killer addiction?"

In one of his books on meditation, *The Orange Book*, Osho suggests meditation called 'Smoking Meditation' for de-automatisation. He says to one chronic smoker, "If Zen people can make a meditation out of drinking tea and make it a ceremony, why not you? Smoking can be as beautiful as meditation."

So here is the technique. When you take the packet of cigarettes out of your pocket, move slowly. Enjoy it as there is no hurry. Be conscious, alert and aware; take it out slowly, with full awareness. Then take the cigarette out of the packet with full awareness, slowly — not in the old hurried way, unconsciously and mechanically. Then start tapping the cigarette on your packet — but very alertly. Listen to the sound, just as Zen people do when the samovar starts singing and the tea starts boiling... and enjoy the aroma.

Smell the cigarette and the beauty of it. Then put it in your mouth, with full awareness; light it with full awareness. Enjoy every act, every small act, and divide it into as many small acts as possible, so you can become more and more aware.

Then take the first puff: God is in the form of smoke. Hindus say, "*Annam Brahm*"—'Food is God'. Why not smoke? All is God. Fill your lungs deeply — this is *pranayama*. I am giving you the yoga for the new age! Then release the smoke, relax, take another puff and go very slowly.

If you can do it, you will be surprised at the stupidity of it. Not because others have said that it is stupid, not because others have said that it is bad. You will see it for yourself. And the seeing will not just be intellectual. It will be with your total being; it will be a vision of your totality. And then one day, if it drops, it drops; if it continues, it continues. You need not worry about it.

Osho says, "This is the secret of de-automatising. If you are walking, walk watchfully. If you are looking, look watchfully, and you will see that the trees are greener than they have ever been and that roses are rosier than they have ever been. Listen! Somebody is talking, gossiping. Listen attentively. Let your whole waking activity become de-automatised." Think and then write.

The Mirror of Consciousness

There's a famous story told by Mevlana Jelaludin Rumi. Once, a great emperor called the greatest artists of his time to create the ultimate throne room. He prepared two rooms, divided by a curtain. On one side sat the greatest artisans of China while on the other sat the best creators from Greece.

The Chinese, with their extraordinary technique and skill, created an elaborate and ornate room befitting the emperor. In the other room, the Greeks laid white marble on the floor and walls. Once the rooms were done, the emperor took a peek into them.

The Chinese room was done in rich brocade, gold and finery. On the other hand, the room prepared by the Greek artists was so well polished that it reflected everything in the other room, while remaining completely empty.

This story signifies the process of meditation and its ultimate realisation of truth. Polishing the marble denotes removing dust — that of thoughts and imagination related to our past from our consciousness.

Osho says, "Your consciousness has to be cleaned, emptied, so you can become a pure mirror, reflecting reality. To be able to reflect reality is to know God, who is just another name for reality."

So how does one clean one's consciousness? Watch and witness whatever you do. Simply sit and watch your body, thoughts and emotions. Witness your whole being from within. Witness that you are not the body. Witness that you are not the mind. Understand that you are only a witness; mere, pure consciousness. And once you realise this, you get in touch with your eternal life and your immortal being.

Freedom from Fear

There's a famous story about a man walking at night and slipping from a rock. Afraid that he would fall thousands of feet below, because he knew that place was a very deep valley, he caught hold of a branch that was hanging over the rock. At night all he could see was a bottomless abyss. He shouted; his shout echoed back — there was nobody to fear. You can imagine that man and his whole night of torture. Every moment there was death, his hands were becoming cold, he was losing his grip... and as the sun came out, he looked down and laughed; there was no abyss. Just six inches down below was a rock. He could have rested the whole night, slept well — the rock was big enough, but the whole night was a nightmare.

Osho says, "From my own experience I can tell you — that fear is not more than six inches deep. Now it is up to you to decide whether you want to go on clinging to the branch and turn your life into a nightmare, or you would like to leave the branch and stand on your feet."

This is the story of our fear, which is deep-rooted in our unconscious. And the unconscious mind is really very heavy. Psychologists say that man is not only his conscious mind; he has also the unconscious layers of mind, nine times more than the conscious. We experience the weight of this mind during our sleep — and in the sleep it feels so real. We get so deeply identified by this that we start sweating and it wakes us up. And then we find that there was nothing to fear.

There's actually nothing to fear. As long as we have the load of our unconscious mind, there's going to be fear in our life. Meditation means we penetrate into this phenomenon of fear and observe it deeply because this observation makes us free. Freedom from fear is the real freedom.

The Bliss of Eternal Now

Our mind is a very strange mechanism. It is an unstoppable manufacturer of thoughts, which are either of the past or the future. And they are a source of tension — the past pulls us backwards while the future pulls us forward. The mind does not know how to remain in the present moment. Actually, the present is not a tense, though it exists in our language. The present is a space of no tenses, no tension between the past and future tenses. It is a space of an eternal now. Meditation takes place in this space.

A meditator gets momentary flashes in this space in the beginning and they are a joy, while a *siddha* or an enlightened being becomes permanently settled in such a space of eternal now.

When Jesus Christ was asked the definition of the kingdom of God, he replied, "In my kingdom of God, there shall be time no longer."

This is a unique definition, but very significant. The Buddhists, Hindus, Jains and Christians may have their theological differences about all other dimensions of their religions, but on the description of *nirvana*, *moksha*, self-realisation or the kingdom of God, they seem to agree on the phenomenon of timelessness.

Osho elaborates about the phenomenon of past, present,

future and the dimension of timelessness: "And when yesterdays are gone and tomorrows are gone, where is today? It exists between the two. If both the banks have disappeared, the river itself will disappear. If both the banks have disappeared, the bridge will disappear. Chunk by chunk in three pieces, time dissolves — first the past, then the future, and finally the present. Then you are left with no time, only a state of timelessness. And this, Buddha says, is *nirvana*.

"To experience timelessness is to experience deathlessness. To experience timelessness is to experience that which really is. It is neither past nor present nor future; it simply is. It cannot be confined to any compartment or category. You simply experience each moment with tremendous peace and silence and joy. And each moment becomes so fragrant, so alive! Each moment becomes such a benediction that it is impossible to imagine it. It is impossible to describe it. One has to know it to know it; there is no other way. It is not expressible; it is not explicable. It is the greatest mystery... Jesus calls it the kingdom of God. That is a positive way of describing it. And Buddha calls it a state of cessation — all has ceased.

"Anger without consciousness is a destructive force, a suicidal force; it hurts you, it kills you by and by; it is poison. With awareness, the same energy is transfigured to become compassion. The same radiance comes to your face, but not in anger — in compassion.

"The same blood flows, the same chemistry of the body, but a new foreign element has entered into it, and the whole chemistry changes," says Osho and offers a panacea for illness.

What is that medicine? The answer is meditation.

The person who gives us this medicine of meditation is a sage, a seer, a mystic, an enlightened one or a *sadguru*. That's why Buddha and Nanak have also described *guru* as a *vaidya*. A *guru* is a *vaidya* of the inner world. He is an alchemist who knows the science of inner transformation. He transforms the baser metals into gold — the raw energy of anger and lust into finer energies of love and compassion. And in this process, we get rid of what is foreign within our system. Our consciousness, *chaitanya*, *atman* are the real self, and all else is foreign, and to realise our real self, we have to go beyond this crude cover of baser elements of anger, jealousy, hatred, lust and violence. We have to get rid of all intrusions ruling the inner country of our consciousness, which is in the state of deep sleep.

Osho explains: "With unconsciousness you are a base metal; with consciousness you will become gold — you get transformed. Just the fire of awareness is needed. You lack nothing else, everything is there. With the fire of awareness a new arrangement happens. You lack nothing, remember; you have everything that a Buddha needs. Just one thing is missing — and that, too, is fast asleep within you. You just have to awaken it; just a few efforts to awaken, a few efforts to become more alert."

Osho says: "The senses go on pouring into you all kinds of impressions from the outside. Whatsoever you see immediately reaches inside; whatsoever you read reaches inside; whatsoever you hear reaches inside. And your *bodhichitta* is like a diamond covered with layers and layers of impressions. Whatsoever these five senses bring to you is going to be taken away by death, because whatsoever comes from without, death will disconnect you from it. It does not become a part of you; it stays apart. It remains a foreign element in you; it never becomes your nature."

Think Less, Be Happy!

Thinking of anything other than the present leads to confusion. Simplifying life begins by treating the present as a gift. It is to find the poor miserable, but what is surprising is that even the well-heeled seem depressed. This makes us wonder what really causes misery. Why does it not disappear by wealth, health or anything else? Osho's reply is: "Misery exists due to the demand and desire for more. Can you see yourself in a situation where you can stop desiring more? Impossible! All of us can imagine a better situation or condition than what we are in. This means you will be miserable no matter where you are. Even heaven is not enough."

Here's an interesting anecdote from the life of the famous litterateur, Leo Tolstoy. One day, as Tolstoy was walking in a forest, he saw a lizard sitting on a rock, sunbathing. Feeling jealous of the lizard, he spoke to it: "Your heart is beating. The sun is shining. You are happy." And added after a pause, "But I am not."

Osho asks: "Why are lizards happy and man is not? Why is creation not happy? Why is the whole creation in a celebration and man isn't? Why is everything, except man, beautifully tuned to itself and into the whole? What has happened to man? What misfortune has befallen him? This has to be understood because from that very understanding rises the path; from that very understanding you become a seeker; and from that very understanding you are no longer a part of the human disease."

Osho answers himself, "A lizard exists in the present. It has no idea of the past or the future. It's in the here; the now. This moment is enough for a lizard, but not so for man. Here arises the disease. You only get one moment. And whenever you become aware, you must become aware in the 'now'. The past is no more; the future is not yet. We go on missing that which is for 'now'; for that future which is not yet; for that past which is no more."

Osho adds: "Drop the past and the future. What does it mean? It means drop thinking, because all thoughts either belong to the past or to the future. There is no thought for the here; the now. Thinking is unreal — it is either a part of memory or of imagination. The real is an experience."

You can dance, sunbathe, sing, love in the reality, but you cannot think in it. Thinking is always 'about' something, and in that 'about' is hidden the whole misery. In that 'about' go on meandering, never quite reaching the point. The point of all meditation is to be like the lizard, sunning yourself on a rock, to be here and now as a part of the whole, but not trying to jump ahead into the future, or trying to carry 'that' which is no more. Unburdened of the past, unconcerned about the future, how can you be miserable? Suddenly, you reach a different dimension. You go beyond time to become a part of eternity. But you refuse to stop thinking and keep wishing for more, getting stuck like an old record. This is like a young girl who looks perpetually glum. Her friend asks her: "Angeline, what's wrong?"

Replies Angeline: "Oh, it is nothing. A fortnight ago, old Mr Short died. He left me Rs 10,000. Then last week, poor Mr Pilkinhouse died of a seizure and left me Rs 60,000. But this week, nothing!"

Forget the Others, Realise Your Self

What is jealousy? Osho explains this thus: Jealousy means ego; jealousy means unconsciousness. Jealousy means that you have not known even a moment of joy and bliss; you are living in misery. Jealousy is a by-product of misery, ego, unconsciousness. And it is not only about jealousy, remember, it is about all problems including greed....

Somebody comes to me and says, "I am very greedy about money. How can I get rid of this greed for money?"

It is not a question of money. Greed is greed. If you get rid of money, you will become greedy for God; greed will still be there. The night Jesus was saying goodbye to his disciples, one of the disciples asked him, "Lord, you are leaving us. There is one question, and it is in the minds of all your disciples. In the kingdom of God, you will be sitting on the right side of God himself — obviously you will be his right hand. And who will be sitting next to you? Amongst us twelve, who will be second to you? That is the most important thing in our heads. Please say something about it; otherwise, once you are gone, it will be impossible for us to decide and we will be quarrelling and fighting over it."

Now, this is jealousy. What kind of disciples did Jesus have?

As far as my observation goes, Jesus was not very fortunate is his disciples. Buddha was far more fortunate. Never in the whole life of Buddha did a disciple ask such a stupid question.

Remember, if greed about money is dropped, immediately it takes over another object; it gets focused on something else. Take responsibility, and then see how things start changing.

If you take the responsibility, if you think, 'I am responsible, not anybody else,' you will not be angry with your wife. You will not be fighting and nagging; you will not be nasty to her. You will start looking deeper and deeper. And in that search you will become aware. That's what awareness is; that's how one becomes aware.

And when you are fully aware of your jealousy, you will be surprised; you are in for a surprise — when you are fully aware of it — it disappears. It simply disappears, not leaving even a trace behind it.

Bring a little light inside. Meditate a bit. Sit silently, doing nothing, looking inwards. In that stillness you will become aware of yourself and of the whole world that surrounds you. That state is *samadhi*, and to know it is to know all; to be it is to be all.

Meditate for Inner Treasure

Existence pulsates with abundance. It embodies godliness. The Hindi word for God is *Ishwar*. The quality of godliness is *aishwarya*. That is our inner treasure.

We carry within us an infinite treasure of spiritual wealth. There is a vast kingdom of godliness within us; it is immeasurable. To open this window of godliness, we need a password, and that really is 'meditation'.

We are living in the age of computers and robots. Working constantly with these mechanical gadgets, we end up behaving mechanically. And to behave like robots is not human because we do not remain masters of our lives. Some other forces of unconsciousness control us. There is no human glory or grace in such existence.

Osho reminds us: "Bring a little more awareness to your existence. Each act has to be done less automatically than you have been doing it, and you have the key. If you are walking, don't walk like a robot. Don't keep on walking as you have always walked; don't do it mechanically. Bring a little awareness to it. Slow down. Let each step be taken in full consciousness."

Lord Buddha used to tell his disciples that when you raise your left foot, deep down, say, 'left'. When you raise your right foot, deep down say, 'right'. First say it so as to become acquainted with the process. Then slowly let the words disappear, just remember, 'left, right, left, right…'

Osho recommends: "Try it in small acts. Eating, taking a bath, swimming, walking, talking, listening, cooking, washing your clothes…de-automatise all the processes. Remember the word: 'de-automatisation'. That is the secret of becoming aware. The mind is a robot. The robot has its utility; this is the way the mind functions. You learn something; when you first learn it, you are aware. For example, if you learn to drive a car, you are very alert. After all, it is dangerous; you have to be aware. But the moment you have learnt driving, awareness is not needed. The robotic part of your mind takes over." And that's when you lose consciousness.

Meditation means regaining consciousness and transcending the robotic mind. Such transcendence happens within the realm of our inner being, our consciousness. Osho says, "The mind opens outside while meditation opens inside. The mind is a door that leads outside to the world; meditation is the door that leads you to your interior, to the innermost shrine of your being. And suddenly, you become enlightened."

The Joyous Adventure of Meditation

Is meditation mere contemplation? No, it is transcendental. It is not about the body or mind or feeling. It is a harmony of all three.

Man is a thinking animal. Thinking is both a blessing and a misfortune. The capacity to think makes one a human. But then man's mind is continuously attacked by thoughts. He has no choice. Thoughts keep coming from all directions, and he has no control over them. He is clouded, even enslaved, by them. He has no freedom. His sky of consciousness remains overcast with thoughts.

There's a famous saying: 'I think, therefore I am.' People have believed this to be a fact. But, in fact, it is neither true nor is it a fact. Our being does not depend on our thinking, though thinking does add another dimension to our being. One can say that thinking becomes possible because of our being. There's no thinking without being, as there's no doing without being. Doing, thinking, feeling are the three dimensions of our being. In our mother's womb, our being existed before we could do, think, feel anything. The being is the foundation on which the human edifice stands. It is the root that makes the tree grow; even blossom. Many think about meditation as something to do with thinking or contemplation. It is not so. Meditation is beyond; it is transcendental. It is not about body or mind or feeling — it is a harmony among all three and goes beyond.

Osho explains: "When you are not doing anything at all — bodily, mentally, at any level — when all activity has ceased and you simply are just yourself, that is meditation. You cannot do it. You cannot practice it. You have only to understand it. Whenever you find time for just being, drop all doing. Thinking is also doing. Concentration is also doing. Even if for a single moment you are just at your centre, utterly relaxed, well that is meditation. And once you get the knack, you can remain in that state as long as you want.

Once a Zen master was asked: "What is the greatest miracle in life?"

His answer was unique. He said: "I sit here all by myself. This experience of just sitting is not of thinking, not of feeling, not of doing — this is pure being."

Osho Upanishad says: "Meditation is a way of settling in oneself, at the core of your being. Once you find the centre of your existence, you have found both your roots and your wings. When you are rooted, you are a more integrated human being, an individual. And the wings are in the fragrance released by being in contact with existence. The fragrance comprises freedom, love, compassion, authenticity, sincerity and a feeling of bliss."

Another insight from the master is: "Meditation is an adventure, the greatest the human mind can undertake. Meditation is just to be, not do anything — no action, no thought, no emotion. You just are and it is sheer delight. From where does this delight come when you are not doing anything? It comes from nowhere — or from everywhere. It is caused because existence is made of the stuff called joy!"

Happy Now, Here!

With every year comes a new year. We greet everyone, mechanically. But nothing changes because there's nothing new. How can we renew ourselves? Why do we want our old letters?

Mulla Nasruddin's former lover asked him. "I've returned your ring. Do you think I'll use your letters to sue you?"

"Oh, no," said Nasruddin, "it's not that. I paid a fellow 25 dollars to write them for me and I may want to use them again!"

This is no joke. It is a deep insight into life. Life is about non-stop repetition.

Unless we learn how to make every morning a new morning, it is not a good morning, even though we would wanted to be so for all those whom we meet. A good morning begins in total freshness when each day a new sun finds something new in us. Unless we feel some freshness in every moment, our so-called new year is not really a new year. We are stuck in our past; our life is as stale as ever.

How can one attain this freshness? Osho says: "Start with this simple method, practicing it at least six times a day. It takes only half a minute, so all you need is three minutes every day. It is the shortest meditation in the world. But you have to do it suddenly.

"Walking on the street, you suddenly think about meditation. Stop yourself. Stop yourself completely. Be still. Be present for half a minute. Whatsoever the situation, stop and just be. Then start moving again. Six times a day at least."

Osho adds: "Look at everything you pass as if for the first time. Make it a continuous attitude. Touch everything as if it is for the first time. If you can do this, you will be freed of your past. The burden, depth, dirt and the accumulated experiences — you will be free of them — every moment, every move from the past.

By constantly being in the present, you will slowly develop an affinity for it. Then everything will be new and you will be able to understand. Meditation tries to get you to live in the present. This technique is one of the most beautiful and the easiest.

If you look afresh even when passing through the same street again, it is a new street. Looking at your wife the way you looked at her for the first time, can you really say that she is not still a stranger? You may have lived with her for twenty, thirty, forty years but are you really acquainted with her? You are like two strangers living together. You know each other's habits and reactions, but the inner core of the being is still unknown, still untouched.

Look afresh, as if for the first time, and you will see the same stranger. Nothing has aged; everything is new. This will bring freshness to your vision. Your eyes will become innocent. Those innocent eyes can see. Those innocent eyes can enter the inner world.

Meditate, Celebrate; Don't Vegetate

You cannot celebrate your life by simply vegetating most of the time. Meditate and nourish yourself by living a natural life.

We live in strange times. A few decades ago, we enjoyed reading great literature — classics of Tolstoy, Dostoevsky, Gorky, Shakespeare, Kalidas. We relished the *Gita*, the *Ramayana*, the *Mahabharata*. We spent hours listening to classical music. We had an educated young generation, culturally rich and thriving. We had time for everything that makes life really rich. Ask any young person today about these things and, in most cases, he will not show any interest in them.

Why? He has no time for all this as he is too busy to competing and surviving in today's world that's moving at mind-boggling speed. He has to do all kinds of odd jobs at odd times that are detrimental to his health. He has to earn a lot to live comfortably with all the attractive technological gadgets. He has little time for anything else. Most of his time is spent on things like sending and receiving SMSs. He has no time to express tender feelings of love in long letters to his beloved. Most of his relationships are really empty, short-lived. There's so much activity and running around but no zest in love. Today's youth is being sucked into unhealthy mechanical jobs, day in and night out, thus deprived of love from family and friends.

Osho reminds us: "People have forgotten the language of commitment, involvement. People don't know the joy of dedication. They don't know what it means to be utterly dedicated to something. It means giving birth to a soul in you. It integrates you, gives you a backbone. People who don't have any experience of commitment — in love, in trust — are spineless and lousy. They are not really human. They have not yet reached that stage.

"To be a man means to be committed, involved, ready to go to the very extreme of some experience. If it appeals to you, convinces you, converts you, then you have to be ready to go wherever it leads you into the unknown, into the uncharted. Yes, there are many fears and challenges, but this is how one grows and matures.

"Millions of people in the world remain immature for the simple reason that they don't know what commitment is. They remain rootless. And when a tree is rootless, you can well imagine what is going to happen to it. Slowly, all the juice will disappear from the tree, because it is no longer connected to anything. The sap will not flow in it, so it will lose its colour and vitality; it will not be young and alive any more. It will lose lustre, grandeur, brilliance; it will lose its luminosity; it will not bloom. Spring will come and go, but it will just remain dead and dry. That's what has happened to millions of people. They have lost their soil… man has lost one quality — zest for life. And without zest, what is life — just waiting for death? It can't be anything else. Only with zest do you live; otherwise you simply vegetate."

Shake off Your Stress

My methods of meditation are ways that will make you expand your energy. Energy is like seeds. One seed can make a whole earth green. One small spark or energy in you can fill the whole earth with dance, song and music. Just a little spark is enough. If you know how to expand it. . . it can become a wild fire. It may be just a little flame within you. Meditation is nothing but an effort to expand your inner flame so that you can become a fire, a flame, a glow, overflowing.

— Osho

"Long-term stress could make people fat," claims a study of around 50 overweight middle-aged Swedish men. Disruptions in the human nervous system or stress can concentrate fat around the abdomen, raising the risk of diabetes and heart problems as found during a study by a university hospital in the Swedish city of Gothenburg.

The Eastern yoga and meditation system offer a perfect solution to this problem. If yoga is too arduous for people, there is Osho's *kundalini* meditation. We recommend this method to be practiced daily for 21 days to obtain marvellous results. It has been effective at Osho centres worldwide. In 1998, a special survey revealed that people all over the world, specially in USA, suffered from Internet depression. The news agency, AFP, circulated the story about *kundalini* meditation as a cure for Internet blues. The report said, "A body under stress creates a surplus of one hormone which stimulates a fat-gathering enzyme. This enzyme is more easily taken up by the abdomen than the other parts of the body. After a long period of stress, the surplus hormone decreases but the fat remains, particularly around the bellies of modern men who do less physical exercise to survive than their forefathers."

Yoga is based upon research. People who live an emotionally suppressed and unsatisfied life eat more, accumulating stress and fat in their body. This can be cured with cathartic techniques such as Osho Dynamic Meditation. The first step is vigorous breathing for 10 minutes. The second step includes catharsis for 10 minutes. The third step is to hammer on the coiled energy of the *kundalini* below the *muladhaar chakra*. Then, there are two steps — 15 minutes of silence and celebration. This is powerful meditation to tone the body. Osho *kundalini* meditation lasts for an hour and has four stages of which three are done with music composed under the guidance of Osho. If you would like to try, it is described below. Remember the last stage includes silence. A gong signals the end of the silent period.

First stage: 15 minutes

Loosen up and let your body shake, feeling energy moving up your feet. Let go and become the shaking. Keep the eyes open or closed.

Second stage: 15 minutes

Dance in any manner you like. Let the body move anyway.

Third stage: 15 minutes

Close your eyes and be still, while sitting or standing. Witness what happens.

Fourth stage: 15 minutes

Keep your eyes closed, lie down and be still.

"...Allow the shaking; don't do it. Stand silently and feel

it coming. When your body starts to tremble, help it; don't do it. If you force it, it will become an exercise. Then shaking will be there but just on the surface. You will remain solid, stone-like, rock-like within; you will remain a manipulator, the doer, and the body will just follow. The body is not the question; you are the question."

Stilll Your Inner Self to Control Your Actions

Violence is an effect, an outward manifestation. So is anger and so is evil. A man hoards money or indulges in adulteration. These are merely consequences. We take action inviting a particular result, without understanding the cause. As long as there is a cause, there is bound to be an effect. If the root is not dissolved, the result flowing from it would continue. Anger doesn't happen on its own; behind it lies a particular disposition, and behind that lies the fundamental nature of the person concerned. The inert overcomes the overt. We cannot remove outward evil without bringing about a fundamental inner transformation.

Psychologists have analysed man's essential nature and concluded that a particular nature gives rise to certain tendencies with resultant consequences. All scriptures, too, speak not of mere outward change, but deep inner transformation. I too have posed this question before would-be ascetics, "Is it possible," I asked, "to achieve non-violence or continence or non-acquisitiveness through the effort of one's will?"

They claim that it can be done. We exercise our will. I may resolve to do or not do something. I take a vow, for example, not to lie. But is that any guarantee that I will not tell lies, or give vent to anger? If one could ensure non-violence through mere exertion of one's will, it would be wonderful. One could resolve to remove a particular evil, but a mere resolution does not end it. It would be wonderful if the mere utterance of a word could accomplish results.

Religious thinkers have offered a way out — they suggest disciplining the mind, body and tongue. With discipline comes fulfilment. If the mind is still, non-violence comes into being. If the mind is pure and still, continence follows, and so does non-greed. But if the mind is restless, if it keeps wandering, if it keeps running after various objects, preoccupied with persons and things, how can there be non-violence or continence? If it were so simple, I would urge the whole world to take to monastic life; no one should remain outside the fold. It would be so easy to just say the word and the work would get done! But in reality this is not so. And a spiritual practitioner who tries to go forward without first maturing his meditation, is often obliged to retrace his steps.

THE ORIGINAL FACE

永恒

Dropping the mask and bringing out your original face is the whole alchemy of meditation.

Be Authentic, Be Blissful!

We are what we are, what we are meant to be. Yet we keep pretending to be what we are not; perhaps, can never be. This is the root cause of troubles.

A husband may not feel love towards his wife, but he has to please her to keep peace at home. So he will exhibit love as a need of the moment. When he does this very often, it becomes his habit. The same is the case with the wife. It happens all the time in almost all relationships. Out of compulsion, people have to pretend to be what they are not. This creates a split personality, leads to inner conflicts and to a life of lies. Such a life is seriously sick and lacks real happiness. How can one be happy when living a divided life — the external in conflict with the internal!

Osho tells a symbolic story about Hitler who suffered from deep depression and melancholy, which psychologists said, was due to a hidden inferiority complex. All the Aryan psychologists were summoned. They tried but they couldn't help; nothing emerged from their analyses. So they suggested that a Jewish psychoanalyst be called. Hitler was not willing to be treated by a Jew, but he had to yield since there was no way out. So, a great Jewish psychoanalyst came. He analysed Hitler by penetrating deep into Hitler's mind, his dreams and then suggested, "The problem is not much. Simply repeat one thing continuously: 'I am important, I am significant, I am indispensable.' Let it be a *mantra*. Night and day, whenever you remember, repeat it: 'I am important, I am significant, I am indispensable'."

Hitler said, "Stop! You are giving me wrong advice."

The psychoanalyst couldn't understand this. He said, "What do you mean? Why do you call this 'bad advice'?"

Hitler said, "Because if I say that I would be such a liar [sic] that I cannot believe it. If I say I am indispensable, I know it is a lie. I may say it, but I am a liar!"

Osho explains: "Out of lies, if you repeat something, it will become a lie. Out of fear, if you do something, it will become fear again. Out of hate, if you try to love, that love will just be a hidden hate; it cannot be anything else. You are full of hate. Go to the preachers and they will say, 'Try to love'. They are talking nonsense because how can a person who is full of hate try to love? If he tries to love, this love will come out of hatred: It will be poisoned already; poisoned from the very source. And this is what the misery of all preachers is."

Even the so-called teachers, educationists and moralists do not show us how to be authentic. They simply tell us to change our behaviour without going through the real transformation that takes place only through deep meditation. People are dishonest because they have to become what they are not. Enlightened mystics give us the science of inner transformation and help us realise our true selves. We feel oneness of the inner and outer, the undivided self, the Advaita. For that, one need not seek psychological treatment; one should learn the Eastern way of meditation.

Be authentic and you will be in bliss!

Be Yourself and Just Be

There are billions of people in this world. But everyone, each one of us, wants to become number one. Isn't it hilarious?

Even if you become the country's prime minister or president, you would still feel that you are not number one. You may come across somebody with a very beautiful body — and rarely does one see prime ministers blessed with one! So as far as beauty is concerned, even a prime minister may feel inferior. And a president may feel inferior to those who are superior to him intellectually, who have created great works of literature and art.

Life is a multi-dimensional phenomenon. You may excel in some dimensions, but you may desire to be excellent in all. Now, that is impossible. There are people who want to be number one even in being humble and modest! Imagine somebody being number one as being nobody…

Osho tells a Sufi parable: A great emperor, Nadir Shah, was praying. It was early morning and the sun had not risen; and it was still dark. Nadir Shah was about to embark on the conquest of a new country, and was praying to God seeking his blessings, praying for victory. He was saying, "I am nobody. I am just a servant — a servant of your servants. Bless me. I am going on your behalf. This is your victory. But I am a nobody, remember."

A priest was also by his side, functioning as a meditator between Nadir Shah and God. Suddenly they heard another voice in the darkness. A beggar was also praying, and he was saying to God, "I am nobody, a servant of your servants."

The king said, "Look at this beggar! He is a beggar and he says to God that he is nobody! Stop this nonsense! Who are you to say you are nobody? I am nobody, and nobody else can claim this. I am the servant of God's servants. Who are you to say that you are the servant of his servants?"

Now you see? It's all still there — the same competition, the same stupidity. Nothing has changed. The same calculation: "I have to be the last. Nobody else can be allowed to be the last." The mind can go on playing such games with you if you are not intelligent.

Osho suggests: "Try never to be happy at the expense of another man's happiness. That is ugly, inhuman. That is violence in the true sense. If you think you can become a saint by condemning others as sinners, your saintliness is nothing but a new ego trip. One has to drop this nonsense of competition. One has to be sensible. Understand your limitations and aspire not for what is impossible. Remember, a rose is a rose. It cannot be a lotus; a lotus cannot be a rose. Be yourself and just be! You will be in total bliss."

Discard Emotional Baggage, Be Authentic

Our life exists between two polarities — being and doing — how we are and how we behave. We may be pure in being but what matters is how we act or behave.

If we observe our life, we will see that our behaviour in our daily wakefulness is not authentic. It is full of hypocrisy. When talking to our friends, relatives, even strangers, we hide our feelings and thoughts. We express what will be socially acceptable and not create problems. This way, the entire society lives a fake life.

Osho tells a significant story. A mother and daughter, both walked in their sleep. One night, the mother got up and went into the garden. Soon, her daughter also got up in her sleep and walked into the garden. As soon as the old woman saw her daughter, she shouted, "Bitch! You've taken away my youth. From the time you were born, I started growing old. You are my enemy. If you hadn't been born, I'd still be young!"

When the girl saw her mother, she shouted, "You wicked woman! Because of you, my life has become a bondage. You have always been a rock in the flow of my life. You are a heavy chain on my life!" At that very moment, the cock crowed and they both awoke.

Seeing the girl, the mother said, "Dear! Why did you get up so early? You may catch a cold. Come, let's go inside!"

Immediately, the girl touched her mother's feet, as she did every morning, and said, "Mother! Your health is not good. You shouldn't get up so early. Come and rest!"

Russian mystic George Gurdjieff said that we should not believe what people say in their conscious state of mind, as they always pretend. Whenever a new person joined his commune, Gurdjieff would make him drunk just to see how he behaved when inebriated and unconscious. For him, it was important to know the real person to transform him, as it is important for a doctor to diagnose a patient. Psychotherapists analyse people's dreams; they think people are truer in dreams than in wakefulness. They cannot hide or manipulate anything in their dreams.

But these are unconscious ways. Osho suggests dynamic meditation to come face to face with one's reality. We can breathe so that whatever we have suppressed in our unconscious mind rises to the surface. In catharsis, we can express it fully and become free of it — totally unburdened of emotional baggage. In this baggage, we carry so many unlived emotions. One is always guilty about so many things. Guilt dominates our mind so much that it doesn't allow us to live naturally.

Osho emphasises: "Drop the guilt! To be guilty is to live in hell. When not guilty, you will have the freshness of dewdrops in the early morning sun, of lotus petals in the lake, of stars in the night. Once guilt disappears, you will live a totally different life — luminous and radiant. You will have a dance for your feet and your heart will sing a thousand and one songs. Be free from your emotional baggage and you will live an authentic life of being."

Kabir, the Everest of Consciousness

A man of consciousness has no enemies at all because he has no fear in his heart. Such a man alone can sing songs of love.

Kabir, the great mystic saint of India, was a real rebel. He sang songs of love and devotion, which did not appeal to scholars because Kabir was not educated. He had the ultimate experience of self-realisation, the godliness. He blossomed into a unique individual. Kabir sang songs of going alone on the path of truth. He said: "One who walks alone, he alone finds the truth." Real spiritual growth occurs when one is capable of going alone. It is a flight of the alone to the alone. It is a journey of *hansa* (swan) to the *maansarovar*, the highest lake. It is not lonely on the top but one shines in aloneness, in full glory on the 'Everest of Consciousness'. This is what happened to the mystic Kabir.

Kabir shared his wonderful songs with the people, but the pundits were afraid. They turned hostile, but as far as Kabir was concerned, he knew no enemies. He couldn't have any enemies because there can be an enemy only as long as there is fear.

Osho explains: "Fearless consciousness knows no enemies.

And when one has no enemies, everyone is a friend. Your friends are not true friends; your friendship is a political device. Your friends are friends because of some self-interest, because of some selfishness. When you die, they will not accompany you. When you are in misery, well, they will be nowhere to be found.

"The real test of friendship is in times of crises. Life is so generous that it offers such critical opportunities in abundance that the friendship has to pass through a fire test. Friendship blossoms in unconditional love."

Mulla Nasruddin once told his wife that 50 per cent of his friends had abandoned him because he was on the verge of bankruptcy. His wife asked, "And why haven't the other 50 per cent gone too?"

Mulla replied, "They do not know about it yet. Only those who know, have left."

Your friends stay with you in your prosperity. When they find there are no more dinner parties or that you have become penniless, they will discard you just like a stick of sugarcane from which all the sweetness has been sucked. Of what use is such friendship?

Osho talks about a Sufi *fakir* who always prayed to God, saying, "O Lord, I shall settle things with my enemies myself, but please save me from my friends." Friends are also secret enemies. But Kabir does not use the word in this sense when he says the whole world has become his friend.

As soon as fear leaves you, the whole world becomes your friend. As soon as you cease to fear death, the whole world turns friendly. Until this happens, there's no such thing as a real friend. Till then some people are bigger enemies, some lesser; some are close enemies, some distant; some enemies are your own people, others are strangers — but all are enemies because they all seem to be destroying your life.

The Courage to be Truthful

Our children behave the way we teach them to. The courage to be genuine gives them the courage to be truthful.

There's a beautiful story in *Chhandogya Upanishad* about the period when children were taught by sages in *gurukuls*. A boy named Satyakam asked his mother Jabaala, "Mother, I want to live the life of a student of supreme knowledge. To join the *gurukul*, I need my family name. Please tell me what it is. Who is my father?"

"My son," replied his mother, "I don't know. In my youth when I went about a great deal as a maidservant, I conceived you. I don't know who your father is. I am Jabaala, you are Satyakam, so call yourself Satyakam Jabaal."

So the boy went to Rishi Gautam and requested him to accept him as a student. "From which family are you, my dear?" inquired the great seer.

Satyakam told him exactly what his mother had said, concluding, "Sir, I am therefore Satyakam Jabaal."

Rishi Gautam said, "None but a true Brahmin, a true seeker of truth, would have spoken thus. You have not swerved from the truth, my dear. Indeed, I will teach you that supreme knowledge."

Our children behave the way we teach them to. The

courage to be authentic gives them the courage to be truthful. Jabaala was a rare mother indeed. She had the courage to admit how she had lived and encouraged her child to accept the situation guiltlessly. She accepted that she had loved many men, was loved by many men and didn't know who Jabaala'a father was. A true mother! And the child was brave too. He said as much to the master, repeating his mother's exact words.

This genuineness appealed to Rishi Gautam who said, "You are a true Brahmin."

This is the definition of a Brahmin. A Brahmin has nothing to do with caste. The very word comes from Brahman, meaning 'seeker of God'.

Says Osho: "The first quality of the seeker is to be authentic and not swerve from truth, nor deceive in any way. Because if you deceive others, eventually you will be deceived by your own deception. If you tell a lie too many times, it starts appearing as truth to you yourself. When others start believing in your lies, you also start believing in them.

"Satyakam, who had gone in search of supreme knowledge, did the right thing. He did not deceive the master. So Rishi Gautam accepted him and said, 'It doesn't matter who your father is. What matters is that you are authentic, sincere, unafraid — capable of speaking the truth without feeling embarrassed. Your mother has given you the right name. 'Satyakam' means one whose only desire is truth. You have a beautiful mother, and you will be known as Satyakam Jabaal'."

Jabalpur, the city of Madhya Pradesh, is named after this very Satyakam Jabaal.

What a Metamorphosis!

Ecstasy exists at many levels. The body is the first level. If we have not known ecstasy on the physical level, it is doubtful that we will know any ecstasy on deeper levels of the heart and soul. One has to start from the beginning. The body is the first step on the inner journey. Every child knows bodily ecstasy by instinct and enjoys it till the parents and the society start teaching him the condemnation of his or her natural instincts. The child begins to understand that there's something in him that is not acceptable. And then begins the journey of being unnatural. The more civilised the family is, the more unnatural it tends to become. The further one goes from Nature, the more perverse one becomes.

Most of our illnesses are rooted in our unnatural lifestyles. Neurosis and schizophrenia are the result of not living naturally, not living in harmony within ourselves, not accepting our instincts in their purity. The first and foremost step on the path of meditation is to accept the body, feel the senses and become aware of them in their entirety. We should not create a split between the body and the soul. In reality they are one. The body is a manifestation of the soul and the soul is the invisible body. They are interdependent. Can the soul exist without the body? It may. But how would you know? Can the body be alive without the soul?

No. The body needs the soul to breathe and throb. They

exist together in an indivisible organic unity. This is the meaning of yoga. There is no real duality between the body and the soul — they exist together in Advaita. It is only in our ignorance that there is Dvaita, a duality. This attitude towards our body gives us the right kind of attitude about how to behave with our body. We feel something of the Divine and need to stop mistreating the body. If we consider the body the temple of the Divine, it becomes impossible to misbehave with it or keep it unclean. We know then that this temple has to be kept clean always. Then there is no question of any indulgence in wrong and unhealthy things. The feeling and remembrance of a temple, its sacredness, will make it difficult for us to do anything ugly to our body.

The trouble is that most of us are not taught to feel this way. Generally we are taught to look at our body as something sinful — an abode of all kinds of sins. Religion and rigid morality by preachers are responsible for this. In the beginning, they launch unnatural condemnation from outside and later it becomes an inseparable part of our conditioning.

One of the first things is to drop all this body condemnation and become natural. Have love and respect for it; feel it from within as if you are entering the temple of the Divine, which it is, because it embodies the Divine. Fulfil all its needs in a balanced way. Proper amount of exercise — not something serious, but playful — will set the tone for the day. And live the whole day as consciously as possible — feeling yourself within your body. Generally we sit, stand, walk and talk and move around as if not carrying our body with ourselves. We are mostly dragging it. Consciousness at each moment will bring an unknown grace and elegance to our body. We just have to decide to be conscious, moment to moment, and then see the magic happen!

We will see that the body has its own joys. Do anything and really anything — breathing, swimming, jogging and then sitting silently — you will feel joy within every fibre of your body. Make every atom of your body happy by giving attention to your body. If you don't feel godly within your body, you won't find God anywhere — no matter where you go, be it outside to a temple, a *gurudwara*, church, Mecca or Medina. God resides within you.

Remember that there is nothing wrong in enjoying physical pleasure. If you don't have access to physical pleasure, you may become obsessed with it. This obsession will definitely lead to perversions. Then there begins a downhill journey leading you to hell. The hell is to be at dis-ease with your body. All condemnations and denials to your body work as toxins and poison your being, rendering you unhealthy. Then you are never at ease with your body. This is the real disease.

To be at ease with one's own body is *sahaj* yoga. To be in harmony with one's body is real health. Take the first step of meditation — love your body. Drop all condemnation and accept your body as the greatest gift of existence. The more you accept it, the healthier and more beautiful it becomes. The more you reject it, the more you drag yourself, the more you become a walking corpse. Make your body a temple and not a grave. Live while you are living — full of love and appreciation for your own body. Listen to its needs. Pay total attention and be sincere to it. It will offer you unknown joys and ecstasies. This first step is the right beginning.

Osho reminds us: "The body is the most complex mechanism in existence. It is simply marvellous and blessed are those who marvel. Begin the feeling of wonder with your own body, because that is closest to you. The closest Nature has approached you, the closest God has come to you, is through the body. In your body is the water of the oceans; in your body is the fire of the stars and the suns; in your body is the air; your body is made of earth. Your body represents the entire existence; all the elements. And what a transformation! What a metamorphosis! Look at the earth and then look at your body — what a transformation, and you have never marvelled about it! Dust has become Divine. What greater mystery is possible? What greater miracles are you waiting for? And you see the miracle happening every day. Out of the mud emerges the lotus and out of dust arises our beautiful body."

RISE IN LOVE

永恒

Love is divine. If anything is divine on the earth it is love, and love makes everything else also divine. Whatsoever is touched by love becomes divine. Love is the alchemy of true life, because it transforms the lower metal into gold.

Place Your Flowers of Feelings at God's Feet

The Baul mystics of Bengal are known for singing love songs with full of reverence for the earth. They are deeply in love with life on earth and do not promise any imaginary heaven in the sky. They are the real people who sing real songs.

In one of the poems, a Baul mystic sings:

Commit yourself to the earth;
while on the earth, my heart
if you wish to attain,
the unattainable man.

The 'unattainable man' means the God within us who is the essential man. The Bengali word is *adhar manush*. The unattainable man is not to be attained somewhere in the Himalayas or the heavens but within us, in the deepest core of our being. It is to be discovered in our meditation. And this process of meditation need not be something serious and grim. In fact, it is an outpouring of our gratefulness to the earth and the whole of existence. All the elements of this existence have created us. We have no reason to feel egoistic as we are not in any way separate from this existence. We are the organic manifestation of this existence. To feel one with it, we simply need to come down from the clouds of our head to our heart and follow our feelings.

The Baul mystics sing:

Place at his feet your flowers of feeling
and the prayers of tears flooding your eyes.

Osho extols the nature of these mystics and says: "They are the real people. They say 'the flowers of feelings'. Ordinary flowers won't do. You can pick flowers from the trees and go to the God of your temple and put those flowers there, but God is abstract; the flowers borrowed."

In fact, they were more in tune with God on the trees. You have not made them closer to God; you have killed them. The Bauls say, 'Your flowers of feelings, place at his feet', which means your love, compassion and understanding be placed at God's feet.

In *A Cup of Tea*, his most famous book of letters written to the seekers, Osho reveals: "The secret of all prayer and worship is hidden in the overflow of those tears. They are sacred. God fills the heart of those he blesses with tears of love, and what to say about the calamity of those whose hearts are filled instead with thorns of hate? Tears flowing in love are offerings of flowers at the feet of God and the eyes from which they flow are blessed with Divine vision. Only eyes filled with love can see God. Love is the only energy that transcends the inertia of Nature and takes one to the shores of ultimate awareness."

Main Hoon Na

Relationships are always a big issue in life — the only one. We spend life thinking and worrying about how to relate to others or how deeply or superficially we should involve ourselves with them. We often get into all kinds of entanglements, as each relationship promises pleasure in the beginning before it turns sour. Some create insecurity; others make us dependent.

Some relationships appear so beautiful that we don't want to lose them. We become possessive. Then comes bondage, which leads to suffering and misery. Relationships create extreme reactions in our being — either we become possessive or else beome as escapists. And these extreme situations are not healthy or harmonious. They have nothing much to do with love — they are weaknesses and dependence on others. They keep our mind, heart and emotions in turmoil. They are not nourishing.

Love is real nourishment but it has nothing much to do with the way we relate with people. Love is a pure joy but these relationships suck our life and leave us in anguish. What is the way out then? How to go beyond bondage and misery?

Osho guides us: "My vision of real humanity is of pure individuals relating to each other but not tied in any relationship. They will love each other but not be possessive. They will be sharing all their joys and blessings, but never, ever in their dreams, think of dominating, of enslaving the other.

"My vision of real humanity is of a world consisting not of families, nations or races, but individuals."

He adds: "Going beyond needs, demands, desires, love becomes a soft sharing, a great understanding. When you understand yourself, you really understand the whole of humanity. Then nobody can make you miserable..."

Relationships

Life does not exist in isolation; it exists in inter-dependent relationships. Our relationships exist on many levels of consciousness. We may not be aware that we are not only related to our near and dear ones, but to whatever exists on this planet or universe. We are related to the earth, the air, the sky and the sun, the trees, birds and animals — all forms of Nature. Theirs is an organic unity and connectivity of life. But what matters to us most are human relationships — between the lover and the beloved, the wife and the husband, the mother and the children, sisters and brothers.

We are related to the earth, the sun and moon, the air, the water, the fire and all elements of Nature. Actually we cannot live without them for a single day. Though we are totally dependent on natural elements and have a close symbiotic relationship, like that of a mother and child, it is surprising that we do not feel any attachment with them as we feel in our blood relationships or even with friends. We know that the relationship between the five elements and us are also a part of our blood. They rule our emotions and thoughts, hearts and minds, but it is in our human relationships that we become emotionally involved and where attachment creeps in. We become so entangled and involved that at a certain point of time we cannot live without them. Life seems to be unbearable without them.

Love in all our relationships in its first stage manifests as an attachment. A child becomes possessive of the mother and father, and the same attachment and possessiveness is present between the child and playthings — toys and dolls. As the child grows up and starts falling in love with the opposite sex, the attachment takes a different form. The young person becomes attached to the lover or the beloved and becomes possessive, finding it difficult to live without these relationships. This attachment may go to the level of life and death. We see some people committing suicide when frustrated due to failure in relationships or even killing others in desperation. This attachment shows the intensity or crudeness of love. And for this reason we say that the person has "fallen in love". This certainly is a fall. Today, love exists on such a low level that it becomes an abysmal ditch.

This attachment is not healthy love and does not nourish people. It is a stagnant kind of love that lacks evolution in consciousness. Love evolves only when we grow in consciousness. The element of meditation and consciousness in love makes it refined and sensitivity gives wings to it, helping it to move upward. Then people grow in love. Love is sharing without demanding anything in return. Love knows the joy of giving without expecting anything in return. Love becomes unconditional and helps the other person to rise to the same level.

Falling in love leads to misery, while rising in love leads to bliss in relationships. This love functions with trust and not with fear or a sense of insecurity. Real love knows no insecurity or fear. This love functions in freedom and not possessiveness, as it trusts totally and knows how to let go.

Attachment is very earthy but freedom in love gives wings to it so that it becomes capable of flying high in the sky. True love needs to be rooted in the earth and also needs wings to fly in the sky. It needs nourishment from both the earth and the sky. Love is a multi-coloured rainbow between the earth and the sky. Osho says: "Love is both. It is rich and it is painful; it is agony and it is ecstasy — because love is the meeting of the earth and the sky, of the known and the unknown, of the visible and the invisible. Love is the boundary that divides matter and consciousness, the boundary of the lower and the higher. Love has roots in the earth; that is its pain, its agony. And love has its branches in the sky; that is its ecstasy. Love is not a single phenomenon; it is dual. It is a rope stretched between two polarities."

Falling in love leads also to lust and lust kills love. Osho says: "Lust is greed, lust is attachment; lust is possessiveness. Love needs no possession; love knows no attachment, because love is not greed. Love is a gift. It is a sharing. You have found something; your heart is full. You hanker for somebody to share it with. It is unconditional. You are so full of it that you would like to be unburdened — just as the clouds, which, when full of rainwater, want to come down as rain.

"Sometimes they rain in a forest, sometimes they rain on a hill, sometimes they rain in a desert, but they rain. The fact of where they rain is irrelevant. They are so full that they have to rain. A lover is so full that he becomes a cloud, full of love-water; he has to rain. That raining is spontaneous."

Love is the Whole *Torah*

What is religion in essence? How do people become religious? Do we really need to follow a code of conduct or discipline? The answer to all this is that one should remember that love alone is the most important thing.

Talking on the divine melody of Kabir, one of the most rebellious mystics of all times, Osho explains: "Religion has nothing to do with churches, temples and rituals; religion is born only when somebody pulsates with love. Each individual has to give birth to a religion and unless you have given birth to a religion in you, you are not religious. You cannot join an organisation and become religious; remember, religion is not an organisation to belong to. To be religious, you have to give birth to religion in your innermost core, in your very core. When religion is born there, only then are you religious."

Osho has a beautiful story from Talmud and this he uses to illustrate his point further. Once a heathen, a great Jewish mystic, came to Hillel and cynically asked him: "Teach me the whole *Torah* while I stand on one foot."

It was an impossible task as it takes years to understand the *Torah*. But this cynic insisted, "If you have understood the *Torah*, then give me the gist, the summary, the essentials. While I stand on one foot, you tell me all that is in the *Torah*."

The cynic had already approached many other mystics earlier and they had all refused to entertain him. They said, “This is impossible; the *Torah* needs years of study, a lifelong study. And the *Torah* cannot be condensed into a few sentences; that will be sacrilege.”

But Hillel agreed, and said: “Do not do unto others as you would not have others do unto you. This is the whole *Torah*; the rest is commentary.”

Osho adds: “Love is the whole *Torah*; the rest is commentary. And what is love? Do not do unto others that which you would not like to be done to you. This is the criterion of love: ‘Do unto others that which you would like to be done to you.’ Whatsoever you ask for yourself, allow that to reach others too. Whatever you don’t want to happen to you, don’t let it happen to others. Think of yourself as the very centre of existence. In fact, don’t think of the other as the other: only you are that. And in the other, too, is present the same life, the same song waiting to be sung, the same urge to rise to the divine, the same seeking, the same inquiry, the same throbbing heart, the same agony and the same ecstasy.”

Love Thyself as Thy Neighbour

Have you ever wondered why you exist? How did you come about? Was there any need for you to exist? You are such a miracle! These are quirky questions which have no real answers. But the fact is that you exist — whether anybody wants it or not, whether you can fulfil certain roles or not.

You are a mystery for existence. You have been given this life to live, to create, to celebrate — do everything that is possible. Don't you value this significant opportunity? Or are you not bothered at all?

Most people live their lives as if they are not bothered at all. Life is there: it is taken for granted and it is wasted in the mundane, in unawareness. Such a valuable treasure...and it is not valued at all. So when you wake up in the morning, pause for a while and meditate before you are caught up in the whirlpool of activity. Feel grateful that life has given you one more opportunity to live differently. Feel grateful that in spite of everything you have been doing, existence is still interested in you and wants you to continue.

Have reverence for existence and love for yourself. Existence loves you and needs you. Let your love reach every cell of your being and energise it. Before you start showering love on others, begin with yourself. It is always easier to love others than oneself, because one keeps finding faults with oneself and feeling inadequate. But do you understand that you are present in existence because existence wants you to be there — the way you are. Existence imposes no conditions on you. It loves you unconditionally whether you are a sinner or a saint. It accepts you for what you are — in your totality. The sun, the moon, the stars and everything in Nature accepts you. Learn from Nature and accept yourself.

So when you wake up, just wash your face and look into the mirror. Look at yourself as if you are looking at your beloved, or at a child. Let your heart speak from your eyes and look with wondrous joy at who you are. For a few moments forget everything and be with yourself. These are the rare moments when you can pour your love upon yourself and feel blessed.

This is a meditation to create a new rhythm in your life. Remember such a lovely beginning will certainly make you love everybody. You will breathe love. Your vibes would be that of love. The magnet of love will work wonders and you will get love in return. There can be no other more powerful meditation than love. LOVE IS GOD.

Let Go of Anger

All that anger does is to turn on you and affect your health, your psyche. Meanwhile, he who has angered you has conquered you A friend once asked the renowned Irish-Australian nurse, Sister Elizabeth Kenny, how she managed to stay constantly cheerful. Sister Kenny replied, "As a girl, I would often lose my temper. But one day, when I became angry with a friend over a trivial matter, my mother gave me the sound advice that I will always remember. She said anyone who angers you actually conquers you."

In a street in China, two persons were quarrelling and a crowd gathered to watch. People everywhere enjoy watching such scenes. They may be out on some serious business but when they see people quarrelling, they forget their work and start watching. Violence has great appeal. That is why all the violence, the blood and gore on television, sells like hot cakes.

Well, one of the Chinese men was rather provoked and spat on the other person. Within minutes, the crowd of watchers dispersed. In China, they believe that the person who spits on the other person first shows his weakness. Because he gets provoked in a quarrel means that the other has been successful in conquering him. The other person has aroused some poison of anger in him, compelling him to spit.

And the anger ultimately hurts the person who gets angry; the receiver of anger may not really get hurt.

One really doesn't have to be a scientist or a researcher to understand the ill effects of anger on one's health. One has only to be sensitive. The being of an angry person starts transmitting anger and violence. Just standing close to such a person may make you feel nauseated. His very presence can be uncomfortable. On the other hand, when you meditate, you feel uplifted and enveloped in a sense of comfort, of well-being.

Exhale deeply and vomit out your anger; not on others but in the emptiness around you. Deep cleanse yourself. The *Atharva Veda* says: 'Cast off anger from your heart, like an arrow from the bow, so that you may again be friends and live together absolutely in harmony.'

Osho concludes: "Tensions are our guests; we invite them. Relaxation is our nature; we don't have to invite it. You don't have to relax; you have just to stop inviting tensions, and relaxation begins on its own. In your very core, in every fibre, in every cell of your being, relaxation percolates and assimilates. This relaxation is the beginning of meditation."

Learn to Live and Celebrate

Remember the eternal truth: 'Weep and you weep alone; laugh and the whole world laughs with you.'

It is your choice what you want to do with your life and how you want to lead your life. You always find yourself on the crossroads and are compelled to make a choice. You may choose out of helplessness, or make a conscious choice. In helplessness, you settle for your weakness, while a conscious choice requires a certain amount of courage and self-confidence, a feeling that this existence is your mother; this universe is your home. This depends on what you nurture in your heart. It is not just a matter of thinking but of feeling — a strong feeling.

In his discourses, Osho exhorts us to nourish our being with positive feelings and embrace life with gratefulness and gratitude. This is the secret of the art of living — and living consciously. The art of living needs a conscious choice. It is not about drifting unconsciously. One is not as weak as one starts assuming in a state of misery. One carries within oneself a vast treasure of godliness. One has to tap it. And the art of tapping is what meditation is all about. Then life becomes a celebration, a carnival of joy. You sing and dance and you find the whole universe singing and dancing with you.

"When thousands and thousands of people around the

earth celebrate, sing, dance ecstatically and are drunk with the Divine, there is no possibility of any global suicide. With such festivity and such laughter, sanity and health, naturalness and spontaneity, how can there be a war? ...Life has been given to us to create, to rejoice, to celebrate. When you cry and weep, you are alone. When you celebrate, the entire existence participates with you. Only in celebration, do we meet the ultimate, the eternal. Only in celebration, do we go beyond the circle of birth and death."

Osho tell us how to be free from pain and anguish: "This pain is not to make you sad, remember. That's where people go amiss. This pain is just to make you more alert, because people become alert only when the arrow goes deep into their hearts and wounds them. Otherwise they don't become alert. When life is easy, comfortable, convenient, who cares? Who bothers? When a friend dies, there is a possibility. When your woman leaves you alone, you are lonely on those dark nights. You have loved that woman so much and staked all, and suddenly you find her gone one day. Crying in your loneliness, those are the occasions when, if you use them, you can become aware. The arrow hurts: it can be used. The pain is not to make you miserable; the pain is to make you more aware! And when you are aware, misery disappears."

Roses and Thorns of Love

Love knows no jealousy. Love is deep understanding. If you love someone, it does not follow that the other loves you too. Love is not a contract.

Love is in the air, as every Valentine's Day sees it. Love has become quite fashionable and there's nothing wrong with that. Young people are becoming passionate about it and soon you will see priests and politicians becoming moralistic about it. People who cannot love become antagonistic towards those who can. There are attacks on love from external forces and there is a lot of internal challenge that love has to face. And one can be totally certain about the possibilities of possessiveness and jealousy creeping in when love happens between two immature people. These things happen in the name of love and they hide behind it. Love is not all roses; there can be many thorns hidden in it.

Osho asks, "But why do they hide behind love?"

Because they feel love is a genuine coin, and you can pretend to be one too when you hide behind it. You can be safe behind love. Whenever you hide yourself somewhere, it simply shows that you consider that place protected; it can become an armour around you. Why does everything seek to hide behind love? Because love is the greatest protective force in the world; the greatest energy in the world. Everything else is false — love is true. All that is not love is false, and whatsoever you do which is not love is a sheer waste. All that is love is true, and whatsoever you do on the path of love increases your being, gives you more truth and makes you truer. Knowing this, everything hides behind love because love can protect. Love is so beautiful that even ugly things can hide behind it and pretend to be beautiful.

Osho quotes an extract from Shepard's *Beyond Sex Therapy*. Shepard was in love with a young woman. Some friends came to see him, but all the time he stayed with the woman and talked to her, he wasn't interested in anyone else. They felt offended and told the woman, "We know Shepard better than you. He has been in love with many women, and this comes and goes. So remember, sooner or later, he will get interested in someone else. What will you do then?"

The woman said, "I will feel jealous, but that is my problem, which I will have to tackle and overcome. But I would like my man to know every type of love, to know all that is possible before he dies, because once gone, one is gone forever. I would like him to live as richly as possible. If any problems arise, like jealousy, they will be mine."

This is true love. It knows the distinction between itself and jealousy. It is not confused. Jealousy cannot hide behind it; it cannot pretend to be love. Osho concludes that love knows no jealousy, no complaint. Love is a deep understanding. That you love someone does not mean that the other should love you also. It is not a contract.

In Love with Existence

For a Sufi, God is his beloved Laila, and he is her Majnu. Love is totally romantic. He sings, he dances. This is his actual prayer.

What is Sufism? It is a love affair with godliness — the ultimate source of all humans and other beings. This existence pulsates with godliness. A Sufi feels this pulsation in his heart. He may not do traditional worship yet he remains thrilled with this pulsation. He sings; he dances. He embraces humans, hugs trees and bows to the sky, the stars. This is his actual prayer.

You must have heard the beautiful Sufi legend about Majnu and Laila. It is not an ordinary love story. The word *majnu* means 'mad', mad for God. And Laila is the symbol of God. Sufis think of God as the beloved; Laila means the beloved. Everybody is a Majnu, and God is the beloved. And one has to open one's heart; the eyes of the heart.

Once a learned Mohammedan asked Osho: "You are not a Mohammedan. Why do you speak on Sufism?"

Osho said, "I'm not a Mohammedan but I'm not a Sufi either. A Sufi need not be Mohammedan. A Sufi can exist anywhere, in any form because Sufism is the core of all religions. Sufism can exist without Islam. It means a love affair with God. One is ready to dissolve into the whole. It is not confined by dogma or creed. Sufis have a special word — *silsila*. What Hindus call *parampara*, they call *silsila*."

One does not have to go anywhere to look for Laila — one has to simply activate one's heart and find her there, in all her beauty. One has to stop seeking outside. *Dil ke aaine mein hai tasveer-e-yaar, jab zara gardan jhukai dekh li* (one has to turn inward, the beloved is right there!)

In *Beyond Psychology*, Osho tells a Sufi story. A young man seeking truth finds an old man beneath a tree. The young man knew that he had to leave on a pilgrimage — but to where? Seeing the old man, he thought, 'He must know the way.'

So he asked the old man.

The old man instructed, "Follow this road till you come to a tree (describing the tree in detail — its leaves, fruit, everything) and you will find an old man like me but 30 years older. He will be your guide."

The pilgrim was happy. He thanked the man and rushed on. For 30 years, he wandered but the tree and the old man never came. He was tired and older himself. Finally, he decided, 'It is better to go home. God knows when the guide meets me; what guidance it will be!' He turned back. He passed the same old tree and was shocked! It was the same man, but 30 years older. The young man said, "My God! Why did you waste my 30 years?"

The old man said, "Did I waste your 30 years, or did you waste mine? Then you were not ripe enough to be guided. You didn't look at the tree, though I described it in detail. I described your guide. You were in a hurry. But I actually waited, knowing one day you will come."

Love and Relationships

It is really mysterious that each relationship begins in the freedom of love and ends in the bondage of a relationship. Love comes like a strong breeze and carries away lovers to unknown dimensions. Lovers go through peak experiences and then need to settle. In the process, they start feeling bored; craving for the same peaks again. When this does not happen, they feel frustrated and fall into the ditch of misery.

Life functions in polarities and dualities. One who understands this is at ease with them and finds peace. By choosing, you end up in misery. Be in choiceless awareness. You attain equanimity and go beyond misery. Osho says that a relationship that is alive is always changing. It has many climates, many moods. It has many surprises. A dead relationship remains stagnant. It is repetitive; it is the same, but then it is no longer a relationship. Then you are not two persons; you just happen to be together.

A relationship based on love and not any business will flow and be river-like. The mystic Heraclitus says, "One cannot step in the same river twice." Alive love relationships come to fruition, but they are never complete. Completion simply means death and nothing else.

In the *Book of Wisdom*, Osho explains the difference between love and relationship, particularly the relationship that we know. He says, "A relationship means something complete, finished, closed. Love is never a relationship; love is relating. It is always a river, flowing, unending. Love knows no full stop; the honeymoon begins, but never ends. It is not like a novel that starts at a certain point and ends at a certain point. It is an ongoing phenomenon. Lovers end, love continues. It is a continuum. It is a verb, not a noun."

A life full of love is not static; it is vibrant. There's a breeziness of freedom in love. Such love knows no bounds, no misery. It is all joy and bliss.

NOW HERE

永恒

This process of watching is the very alchemy of real religion, because as you become more and more deeply rooted in witnessing, thoughts start disappearing. A moment comes when there is no thought at all. You are, but the mind is utterly empty. That is the moment of enlightenment. That is the moment when for the first time you become unconditioned, sane, a really free human being.

Be Happy in Others' Riches

Jealousy isolates us. Unknowingly, we bond with the person we are jealous of and we become belligerent, competitive, unhappy, discontented and self-destructive.

Behaviourists attribute comparison to be the major cause of people's unhappiness in the developed world today. People are happy when they grow rich as individuals, but not as a society. They "were happy with less, as long as they were better off than others." Moreover, because others "work harder to earn more money and spend more, their happiness diminishes." In order to consume more material goods, they tend to work harder, and so have little leisure.

The other reason is 'habituation'. Economists say the effect of happiness fades rapidly. What was a luxury in the past becomes today's need. These are the findings of a survey conducted at Harvard University by Professor Richard Layard who calls them "a form of pollution". Moreover, these students are brilliant youngsters who, in a few years, excel in their professions and influence global opinion, but for now, they cannot discriminate between having enough and greed.

The A&M and AC Nielsen survey on a small number of young economically elite from Indian metros revealed that educational qualifications apart, they measured their social status with cars, posh residential addresses, overseas trips and latest gizmos. Generation X is chasing the new *mantra:* "I must own what the rich possess." Clearly self-fulfilment is rudimentary.

Mystics attribute this kind of unhappiness to the universal negative emotion called 'jealousy'. *Webster's Dictionary* too defines jealousy as the apprehension of being displaced by a rival and/or to be revengeful on this account. Fear causes jealousy — a destructive force. It arises when we distrust and suspiciously watch others and are envious. The happiness of others causes jealousy, which turns into misery. On the other hand, positive emotions, such as love and joy, are dynamos of energy.

As a by-product of unconsciousness, jealousy isolates us. However, neither repression nor aggression is beneficial. Suppressing pain in the body, won't help. It will surface, sooner or later, as a health or a psychological problem. It is, therefore, important to cleanse such emotions rather than ignoring or suppressing them. Yoga, exercising and jogging help one to release negative emotions.

A beggar once complained that he was unhappy because he possessed nothing. The king was a wise man. He called him and offered him Rs 1 lakh for one arm. Shocked, he refused. The king raised the offer to Rs 2 lakh for both arms. The beggar did not agree. The king similarly bid for various parts of the beggar's body, but the beggar said 'no'. The king reminded him of his earlier statement and asked why he was not availing the opportunity to possess wealth. The beggar realised that his strong body was more important than other people's wealth.

Similar experiences transform us. But does the effect last? Sooner or later, we return to our old behaviour pattern, even though we have been told since our childhood that jealousy can be transmuted into love. Here is a meditation technique that can be done independently. All it needs is one's total commitment. Don't repress it; express it. Sit in your room, close the doors, and bring your jealousy into focus. Watch it, see it, let it acquire as strong a flame as possible… burn in it and see what it is. And just let the jealousy be there. Look deep into it and do likewise with anger; do it with sadness, hatred and possessiveness. And by and by, you will see that just by seeing through things, you start getting a transcendental feeling that you are just a witness… The identity is broken only when you encounter something within you.

All our moods are transitions that leave us in constant chaos. To transcend the dual emotions, including sadness and joy, anger and peace, hate and love, it is essential to witness the pair. These dualities co-exist and cannot be transcended in isolation because when we watch one, we cannot see the other, which surfaces and traps us. To transcend hate, love has to be transcended. Diminishing jealousy does not work. Osho says, "If you diminish your hate, your love will disappear — that's what has happened. You have been taught not to hate and the total result is that you have become incapable of love."

Most of all, it is important to participate in the happiness of others. Osho says, "Just by being happy with happy people, you create a situation in which your own inner flower starts blooming." So, open your heart. Although difficult initially, it works and jealousy stops having an impact on our lives.

Further, mystics say unhappiness is a result of turning away from oneself. This creates a vacuum, which we try to fill with indulgence as a means to happiness. However, materialism gives a reflection of fleeting happiness. It is a flirtation. The richer a man becomes, the unhappier he is because he yearns for more. Ownership of material goods gives him power and unknowingly he is sucked into endless competition.

Accepting pleasure as happiness results in a vacuum and remorse, just as the Buddha had said, "Desire is difficult to fulfil." Moreover, competition and jealousy do not lead to happiness. On the contrary, a positive attitude of being happy promotes well-being and harmony.

Spirituality of Money and Love

For long India has been considered a poor country. This is a fact even today, though it now has a sizeable middle class. This may be music to many ears but there's better news.

India is the richest in spirituality. The same is becoming evident to the world. I do not want to sound nationalistic; for me, it is just the recognition of a fact. Despite the presence of a large number of religious fundamentalists, India continues to be the right place for spirituality.

During my recent visits to West Asian countries, I did not find any Sufis. Their presence was not so visible even in their place of birth. But here in India, Sufism is spreading. Buddhism is thriving and Jainism is also attracting people. There are Bhakti festivals of Hindus, Sikhs and Christians all through the year. In a nutshell, spirituality is flourishing like never before.

Besides, the new generation is coming up with different kinds of spiritual packages like The Art of Living, The Art of Relaxing, The Art of Being and The Art of Loving. They seem to be diluting spirituality to make it more acceptable and saleable. Though all these are not exactly spiritual — they seem rather commercial, but are based on demand and supply.

Says Osho in his Zen discourse under 'No Water, No Moon': "There are only two ways to live your life, only two ways to be: one is the right way, the other is the wrong way. The right is to give, to share and to love. The wrong is to snatch, to exploit and to accumulate. Love and money are the symbols of these two ways. Love is the right way and money is the wrong way. When love becomes artificial, money becomes important."

Can You Patent a Rose?

Spirituality, a science of inner transformation, is universal in nature. It is nothing but sharing wisdom, consciousness and love with everybody. Such spiritual people have been travelling the world over to enlighten and raise the level of consciousness in humanity.

Swami Vivekananda and Swami Ramteerth went to the US and shared their wisdom and meditation. They gave it free. But these days Indian yoga teachers go West to sell Eastern wisdom and knowledge at a high price. They change little in the West, but the West changes them totally. A couple of years ago, I saw a news item in various newspapers which was extraordinary:

'Bikram Choudhury, a former weightlifter based in Los Angeles, is being sued over his claim to own the copyright of a series of 26 postures used in Bikram yoga, a fast-growing style in which exercises are repeated in a studio heated to 40°C.' The article continued, 'Mr Choudhury has sent letters to more than 100 Bikram Yoga Schools and teachers, accusing them of violating his copyright and trademark by deviating from his strict teachings and employing instructors who were not trained by him.'

"In response, a collective of US yoga teachers are suing Mr Choudhury in a San Francisco federal court, arguing that his copyright and trademark claims are unenforceable, because his teachings draw on postures in public use for centuries."

It is stupid to impose a trademark on yoga postures and meditation methods. I wonder why we don't do the same with postures of the *Kamasutra*! What would happen if a dancer gets the trademark and copyright over postures of Bharatanatyam, Kathak and Odissi dance forms? People have a trademark for The Art of Living and The Art of Being; why don't they have a trademark over breathing and *vipassana* too?

Breathing, *yogic* or otherwise, has been happening since eternity. Lord Shiva taught this to his consort Parvati — not only a single technique, but 112 methods of meditation. *Vipassana* is only one of them. Luckily, the Buddha did not get a trademark or copyright, so we continue doing *vipassana* without fear.

But in the US all kinds of things are possible, and it is becoming prevalent in India too. In one discourse on '*Om Shanti, Shanti Shanti*', he says: "Things can be copyrighted, thoughts cannot be copyrighted, but meditation cannot be copyrighted. They are not things of the marketplace. But, perhaps the West cannot understand the difference between an objective commodity and an inner experience."

Osho says further: "Maharishi Mahesh Yogi copyrighted transcendental meditation. Underneath, in a small circle, you will find the words TM!"

Osho told his secretary, Ma Neelam, to write to such people, "You don't understand meditation. It is nobody's possession. Perhaps, if your country gives trademarks and copyrights on meditation, it will be good to have a copyright on stupidity too. Only you will be stupid, not anybody else. It will be illegal."

Time to Herald a New Humanity

The most important need of humanity today is to be made aware that its past has betrayed it. There is no point in continuing with the past, for doing so will be suicidal. The new humanity will not be a society in the old sense, where individuals are only part of it. It will be a meeting of individuals, where individuals are the masters and society is there to serve them. It will have many different aspects to it — it will not have so many religions; it will have only a religious consciousness.

The individual, for the first time, will not be programmed; he will be helped to be himself. He will not be given any ideals or discipline, nor any certain patterns. He will be given only tremendous love for freedom so that he can sacrifice everything — even his own life, though he cannot sacrifice his freedom. He will not be repressive; he will be natural, with no inhibitions, expressive of everything that he has, just as plants express themselves in different colours and fragrances.

The new individual will not be under the illusion that all human beings are equal, for they are not. That each individual is unique is a far higher concept than equality. Although the new individuals will not be 'equal', they will have equal opportunities to develop their potential. There will be no marriage; love will be the only law.

The new humanity will have an ecology in which Nature is not to be conquered, but lived and loved. We are part of it — how can we conquer it? It will not have any race, nation, state, colour or caste. It will have only a functional world government that will not be chosen by mediocre voters — because they necessarily choose people of their own category.

The new humanity will have a totally different pattern. Unless everyone is well educated and has at least a bachelor's degree, he will not be allowed to vote. There will be a no-party system because people will vote directly for individuals. The government, unlike at present, won't have any power; it will be simply functional. It will serve society in the real sense; not just in words.

Life has so many dimensions, but politics has dominated them all. Looking at a newspaper, someone on another planet would find it difficult to conceive what kind of people live on earth — only politicians? Murderers? Rapists? Criminals? Because media reports cover only these people and on top of everything is the politician.

Every creative dimension of life will be brought to light, and the ugly aspects will not need to be advertised. If somebody commits a murder, it should be brought to light — not to say that he is a criminal, but to show how the very psychology of the man, his upbringing, has gone wrong, and why he was forced to commit murder. In his place, with the same background, anyone would have done the same. So why are you not condemning the person? You are condemning the training, the background, the upbringing — that is absolutely scientific.

Newspapers should be full of creativity and positivity. Ninety per cent of newspapers should give coverage to musicians, poets, sculptors, dancers, actors, philosophers and only 10 per cent should be given to politicians and the negative elements. The negative elements should be analysed so that the individual is not condemned. And politicians should only be given space for conveying information; no more. If they are doing something good or bad, it should be reported — but they should not dominate our entire lives.

A Holy Land is Nobody's Property

The famous social worker and Magsaysay award-winner, Anna Hazare, feels that neither a *mandir* nor a *masjid* need be constructed at Ayodhya as there is no dearth of them in India. What matters is a positive change in human attitudes. Famous poet-and-filmmaker Gulzar suggests that a university or a mosque be built instead. Mahashweta Devi, author and winner of the prestigious Jnanpith Award, has a similar feeling. Kiran Bedi is all for a Nature Park, while author Nayantara Sehgal votes for a meditation space. Former Miss India, Celina Jaitly, wants that we should build a school where children, irrespective of which community they belong to, can study together. There are also the regular pro-*masjid* voices like that of Mulayam Singh Yadav and pro-*mandir* voices like that of the leaders of Vishwa Hindu Parishad. Famous historian Mushirul Hassan would like a Gandhi memorial so that the site may become the Kaba and Kashi for those with in a stake in our democratic and secular fabric.

Known as the most prolific thinker of the 21st century, Osho, in an interview to Pritish Nandy in 1989, spoke on this subject. In the light of the recent and not so recent developments that have taken place, it might be interesting to read Osho's opinion on the issue. Read on:

Question: There is this issue of secularism, and there is a great controversy going on regarding the Ramjanambhoomi and the Babri Masjid in Ayodhya. Both the communities, Hindus and Muslims, are claiming that place. How can this issue be defused?

Osho: There is no problem of...There are politicians behind the problem. Otherwise, both can worship at the place; both can make it holy. It is holy to Hindus and to Mohammedans. What is the problem? Israel is a holy land for Christians because Jesus was born and crucified there. It is the holy land for Jews because Moses founded the country. It is holy for Mohammedans because when Mohammed went to heaven, riding on his horse, he stopped for rest on a rock in Israel. So that rock is a problem. And I don't see any problem. All can worship a rock. The rock will not say, "No, you cannot worship me."

It simply has to be made clear to them that the whole earth is holy. And if you think this part is holy for you, you should be happy that this part is also holy for the Hindus and for the Mohammedans. You should invite Christians, Jains, to make it more holy. It is sheer childishness to fight on these problems; but, politicians gain power only when fights go on. Now the government will be in difficulty. If the government sides with the Hindus, the whole Mohammedan community will go against it in the elections. If the governement sides with the Mohammedans, the whole Hindu community will go against it. So they just talk about it, discuss it in the Parliament but nothing happens and nothing will happen. My suggestion is very simple — a holy land is nobody's property; anybody can worship there. The more people that worship it, the more humanitarian it becomes.

Except Love, There is no God

The eruption of Hindu-Muslim violence in Gujarat was a "disgrace to the nation", said our Prime Minister. Of course it was a disgrace and very shameful too, but there is more to it. It is a disgrace to the religions that people follow. After this cruel massacre of over 600 persons in Gujarat, it would be really appropriate that the so-called religious and political leaders gather at one place together and hang their heads in shame. They must own the responsibility because they are the real culprits of this large-scale violence. It is their leadership that has utterly and miserably failed. They have misled the people. They have interpreted the teaching of their religion in a way that has led to this senseless violence. This venomous indoctrination of the belief-system in the minds of gullible followers is the real cause of what happened in Godhra and the rest of Gujarat.

The first step for these religious leaders should be to feel ashamed and apologise to their followers and admit that they have failed. The second step will be to go through a process of therapeutic introspection, some meditation to cleanse themselves and detox themselves of all communal hatred. Such incidences always compelled Mahatma Gandhi to go on a fast, but today we don't see any religious or political leader (Mahatma Gandhi was both) who does that. Insensate to the core, they have no heart and no compassion. Our country needs to be saved from these so-called religious and political leaders.

Talking about the communal violence, Osho says that it is nothing new in India. It erupts almost every 10 years; 10 years seem to be the limit. "Within 10 years, every person accumulates so much violence within himself that it has to find an outlet, otherwise it is liable to destroy him. He will be burnt up by his own violence. So he has to find some excuse — political, religious and social — any kind of excuse will do. And this limit of 10 years is not only limited to India; it seems to be universal. Every 10 years there is a great war; the whole of humanity gets involved in destruction.

"The responsibility is of the religions, because they have not taught how to love; they have only taught you how to be afraid. Remember, fear is the same energy as love, but it has been poisoned — your energies have been poisoned for centuries. So it has become a routine phenomenon that after a few months, a few years, after a certain period, one accumulates so much violence none of which would have been there if love had been flowing. Because love has been stopped, there is no flow in your life. Your own energies go against you; they become destructive. Then any excuse is enough.

"The real thing is that people are accumulating intense violence, anger, in them. If you cannot release your love, you will accumulate anger. Love, standing on its head, becomes anger, and when anger accumulates, you begin to look for some excuse. If you cannot find an excuse, you invent one; but you will have to invent some cause so you can unwind. This is catharsis — on what grounds it happens is immaterial."

People have gathered so much poison, anger, that these flare-ups are bound to happen. And then politicians have no understanding; they simply go on dumping the whole thing on "anti-social elements", as if these anti-social elements appear only once in a while and then suddenly disappear. They are always there, but the riots are not always there. For years these anti-social elements have been very peaceful and very Gandhian, very non-violent, and then one day suddenly they erupt, and they erupt all over. It is almost like a chain reaction.

The politicians have to say something. They don't understand what is happening at all, and even if some of them do understand, they don't have the courage to admit it.

Osho offers a simple solution and says: "I am absolutely in favour of a new culture arising, a new civilisation arising, a new morality arising, a new humanity arising. Otherwise this country is going to remain poor, starved: continuously fighting, quarrelling, killing each other. This country needs to be taught ways of love. This country needs to be told that except for love, there is no God. Drop all fear! Don't go to the temple because of fear, and don't worship idols and gods because of greed. Drop greed and fear and live out of love — love people, love trees, love animals, love this existence, because God is nowhere else. God is spread all over existence. God is simply another name for life; existence, that's what it is.

Buddha's Message for Bill Gates

Bill Gates must be feeling poorer after being declared number two amongst the richest people on earth and thus busy planning to regain the lost glory of being number one.

According to the *New York Times*, "Microsoft was preparing a broad campaign countering the movement to give away and share software code, arguing that it potentially undermines the intellectual property of countries and companies."

Recently there has been undue concern in Western nations over protection of the so-called intellectual copyrights and trademarks of not only scientific knowledge, but of spiritual and traditional knowledge that is our common heritage.

Scientific knowledge has its own tradition. Osho tells us about this tradition: "...scientific truths, once discovered, become the property of everybody else. Albert Einstein worked hard for 13 years to discover the theory of relativity; now you can read all about it within hours — you need not discover it again. Edison worked for years, at least for three years, to discover the first electric light bulb; now you can go on producing electric light bulbs – you don't need Edisons to produce them. Ordinary labourers, who know nothing of electricity, can do the job – they are doing it.

"Do you know? Where it is all coming from, what Microsoft has it today and what it sells, thereby making billions? It has its roots in the traditional scientific knowledge that has been freely available all along. And those earlier scientists did not make billions. Their inventions and discoveries have been a gift to the whole world. The science of total health of the inner, the *yoga-sutras*, has been freely available to the whole world. Shiva gave 112 techniques of *tantra* and the world has been benefiting from this inner science without ever feeling a need of any trademark or patent.

"We, in the East, believe that whatever comes in the realm of science and knowledge should remain an open source and everybody should be welcome to drink from the fountain of knowledge. Knowledge is a liberating phenomenon. The *Upanishads* declare: '*Sa vidya ya vimuktaye* (knowledge liberates).' True knowledge is of universal nature and is meant for the liberation of mankind."

The media is right in observing that Bill Gates is being stingy in his approach. He is already the richest man in the world but his greed seems to have no limit. Some others in the West have gone to the limit of patenting *neem*, *haldi* (turmeric) and Basmati rice — an act that could not even be conceived of in the East; hopefully it won't be in the future either. Now some misguided people are trying to register the trademark for certain Eastern meditation techniques, especially Osho active meditation.

Osho once said, "I would like you to be enriched by Newton, Edison, Eddington, Rutherford, Einstein and I would also like you to be enriched by Buddha, Krishna, Christ, Mohammed, so that you can become rich in both the dimensions — the outer and the inner. Science is good as far as it goes, but it does not go far enough as it cannot go. I am not saying that it can go and it does not go. No, it CANNOT go into the interior of your being. The very methodology of science prevents it from going in. It can go only outwards; it can study only objectively. It cannot go into the subjectivity itself. That is the function of religion.

"Society needs science; society needs religion. And if you ask me what should be the first priority — science should be the first priority. First, the outer, which is the circumference; then the inner, which is more subtle and more delicate. Science can create the real space for religion to exist on the earth."

About knowledge, he says, "*Sa vidya vimuktaye* (kowledge is that which liberates). This is a marvellous saying. It is the most original definition of knowledge. This is the definition of knowledge as well as its criterion."

Osho was against copyrighting of knowledge and thoughts and said, "Things can be copyrighted; thoughts cannot be copyrighted, and certainly, meditation cannot be copyrighted. They are not things of the marketplace. For 10,000 years the East has been meditating and nobody has put a trademark upon meditation."

(Please note that the above article is based on a news item published a couple of years ago.)

Fathers and Sons

Once I visited a *sannyasin* friend of mine — Swami Kapil. We were busy chatting when Kapil's father came in. I had never met his father earlier, so Kapil introduced me to him, saying, 'Meet my biological father'. I felt embarrassed on hear a statement like that but I saw that Kapil was totally comfortable in introducing his father this way. Visibly, his father also did not feel anything wrong with this statement; maybe, he felt hurt but chose not to exhibit it.

"This incident is 20-years old but is still fresh in my memory, because it sounded very odd. Though it is a fact, but I felt it showed a complete absence of respect for the father.

It is so difficult to show respect towards the father who has always dominated the son in his childhood — that's why the idea of celebrating Father's Day. This day has its origin in feelings of guilt, dwelling deep in sons. Poor father! He does so much for his children but what we often see is an endless conflict between them, especially between fathers and sons."

Osho talks about a great Russian novelist, Turgnev, who has written a book — perhaps a masterpiece — *Fathers and Sons*. The book is about the struggle between fathers and sons, because fathers would like sons to be their replicas.

Naturally, they will not allow sons any freedom. Obedience they expect and they expect their sons to be their carbon copies. He says in this book that the relationship between a father and son is always one of conflict. There is no other tie, except the tie of conflict between them. The son is the rightful successor of the father and therefore, is always engaged in removing him. He waits eagerly for him to vacate his position. The son hates the dominance of the father in family affairs. When this becomes unbearable for the son, he may even go to the extent of killing his father in anger. This conflict is an eternal one and a chapter was recently added to this hate-saga in the shape of royal killings in Nepal a few years ago. If we look at this situation in psychological terms, we come across some startling revelations. Freud did a lot of research on this subject and said that people worship God as a father because at some period of time they must have killed some dominant or dictatorial father, somebody who was too dictatorial. It is a well-known fact that many a king has been killed by his son because the king refused to abdicate, making the heir wait endlessly. The son, on advancing in years, felt that he would never get to be the king; so the only possibility lay in the death of the father. Many kings have imprisoned their fathers and taken over the throne by force on seeing no possibility of the king's death. What would be the point of getting the throne when you are 80-years old when your father dies and you succeed? In a short period of your rule, you would be gone too.

Osho appreciates the psychological insights of Sigmund Freud who says that because somewhere in the past man had been tempted to kill his father, he could not forget the guilt of his crime. And out of that guilt, he started worshipping ancestors, the father, elderly people, and the old. All this respect has arisen out of a guilt that is deep set in the human heart. Man started creating a God who was like a father; raised temples and statues in his memory, appointed priests to help in praying, worshipping and so on. Behind this whole facade and drama of religion, Sigmund Freud finds only one single reason: somewhere in the past man has behaved so badly with his father — perhaps even murdered him — that he has been unable to forgive himself. So the only way is to pray — make God your father, the creator of the world. All these hypotheses, provide an original insight.

Lao Tzu says: "The more you try to make sons listen to their fathers, the more they go against them." And Lao Tzu has been proved correct. In the last 5,000 years, man has tried to make the son obey his father but the outcome has been an increasing abyss between the two. A son touches his father's feet and things of what he will inherit from him. It is said that the sons of rich fathers never lament their father's death. They cannot; perhaps they are happy. The sons of kings have been known to bring about the death of their fathers. All around us can be seen cases of manipulation.

There is no need for the son to agree with the father. In fact it seems far better that he should not agree. That's how evolution happens. If every child were to agree with his father, then there would be no development. Ultimately everybody would have been where God left Adam and Eve — naked, outside the gate of the Garden of Eden. We would still have been there. It is because sons have disagreed with their fathers, forefathers and with their entire tradition that man has evolved.

This entire process of evolution is a result of the sharp disagreement with the past.

Your Enemy Changes You More than Your Friend

We celebrate Diwali with pomp and show. We witness the multi-coloured lights of the lamps dazzle our eyes. Sounds of all kinds of firecrackers are heard at every step. Children enjoy the loud reverberations and derive joy in shocking elderly people with the sound of their firecrackers, specially when they catch them unawares.

To the mature and intelligent, this whole scene of fireworks and sounds is simply a nuisance, noise and pollution. It is unhealthy and risky, as we know these firecrackers can hurt and kill people. This will happen for many years to come, but for just one day in a year. But for the big, rich kids this kind of dangerous Diwali begins many weeks prior to Diwali.

These kids have been detonating bombs in Afghanistan and they think that by bringing darkness and death to the people of this poor country, they can celebrate light in their life. They have the same logic — the logic of their enemy Osama bin Laden, who instigated his followers to kill thousands of innocent people in the World Trade Center.

Laden thought and continues to think that America is evil and must be destroyed at any cost, even if his children have to commit suicide to kill it.

There's a strange rule and mysterious wisdom in life: Your enemy changes you more than your friend. By fighting with your enemy, you become like your enemy. So you can choose anybody as your friend, but you have to be careful about choosing your enemy, because in your fight with your enemy, you are bound to become like him. Already people have started calling these two war heroes as: Bush bin Laden and Osama the Bush. You may have seen Bush with a Mullah-type beard some months ago.

We have also seen this phenomenon among the ruling and opposition parties. Over time, they become like each other, acquiring the characteristics of the other. The Congress becomes a BJP look alike and vice-versa. And we have often prided ourselves that India, though attacked by barbarous invaders, has never ever attacked any country. This pride will soon be shattered if our inimical neighbour keeps offering provocation. The President of our army-ruled neighbour could influence our democratically-elected leaders so much so one day they too may become like him. Our leaders had better watch out.

Osho reminds us of the very significant insightful message of Jesus:

"Jesus says: 'Love thy neighbour as thyself' — again and again and He also says: 'Love thy enemy as thyself.' And if you analyse both sentences together, you will come to find that the neighbour and the enemy are almost always the same person. By saying 'Love thy neighbor as thyself' and 'Love thy enemy as thyself', what does he mean?

"He simply means that do not have any barriers in your compassion, in your love. As you love yourself, love the whole existence, because in the ultimate analysis, the whole existence is yourself. It is you who is reflected in many mirrors. It is you; it is not separate from you. Your neighbour is just a form of you; your enemy is also a form of you. No matter what and whom you come across, you come across yourself. You may not recognise this phenomenon because you are not alert; you may not be able to see yourself in the other because something is wrong with your vision, with your eyes."

Compassion is therapeutic, according to Osho. Meditation leads to compassion and one rises above hate and enmity. "Compassion is an inner air-conditioning. Suddenly everything turns cool and beautiful, and nothing can disturb you. The whole of existence is transformed into a friend. Now there are no more enemies, because when you look through the eyes of anger, somebody becomes an enemy but when you look through the eyes of compassion, everybody seems a friend, a neighbour. When you love, you find God everywhere; when you hate, you see the devil everywhere. It is your standpoint that is projected on to reality."

The Eleventh Commandment

A friend from the US sent me the eleventh commandment, which came into existence after September 11. At a staff meeting in heaven, God, Moses and St. Peter concluded that the behaviour of President Bush and Osama bin Laden had induced the need for an eleventh commandment. They worked long and hard in a brainstorming session to decide on the wording of the new commandment, because it had to have the same style, majesty and dignity as the original ten. After many revisions, they finally agreed that the eleventh commandment should be: 'Thou shalt not sleep with thy enemy.'

This particular insight from heaven revealed the manner in which the two sworn enemies of today had been dealing with each other in the past and doing business with each other.

The other day there was a news item which conveyed that Osma bin Laden's family in Saudi Arabia had snapped its financial ties with the Carlyle Group, which is a politically-connected private investment firm. The news item revealed that Carlyle owned about $14 billion in assets. Its chairman, Frank Carlucci, was a former US Defence Secretary. President George Bush, James Baker, former Secretary of State, and Arthur Levitt, who was Chairman of the Securities and Exchange Commission throughout Clinton's administration, are senior advisers to the firm. On the other hand, the US administration is trying its level best to track down Osama bin Laden for years. But were all the possible avenues explored?

Indeed, it is a known fact that before September 11, the FBI blocked all investigations that came too close either to the Saudi royal family or to bin Laden's family interests. It also became known that they had access to leaked FBI reports. It was stated, "Bush Jr. made his first million through a firm called Carlyle, which was financed by the bin Laden family, and both he and his father were paid by them."

The FBI reported that they were closed down: if so, then what happened to the questions raised by the US intelligence?

It is not merely a question of funding terror, but also of money laundering, Saudi involvement in Nicaragua and various deals help the US to get cheap oil, Saudi princes get to do what they want and George Bush manages to get rich. Some officials in the US State Department also realised that Saudi Arabia is a friendly country practicing a moderate form of Islam, and that the FBI has no understanding of high-level international intelligence. But we all know such liars cannot continue for long. Their lies have become too complex and the world is too small a place to conceal them. An infinite greed for money and power is the root cause of all terrorist attacks. It has nothing to do with religion or *jehad*. The fact is that the warring Bush and Osama have already been sleeping with each other and fooling the world. This is an old marriage of convenience between George the Osama and Bush the Laden.

Key to Liberation

"Every morning when I get up, the first thing I decide is what I want. Is it misery or bliss that you are going to choose today? And it happens that I always choose bliss. It is my choice; it is my life," says Abdullah.

Our life is out of our own choice. Our birth was not of our choice; it was the decision of our parents. They brought us into this world without consulting us or even seeking an approval from us.

We came into this world of Osama bin Laden and Bush without our conscious choice and now we are condemned to live in their world. We cannot wish away these war-mongers, but what we can surely do is to transform our life and bring meaning to our life by making some conscious choices.

How can this happen? How do we drop misery and choose peace and happiness?

The answer is — by being masters of oneself.

In India a *sannyasin* is called a *swami*. Why? Because, he does not let anybody else decide his life. A *swami* makes his own decisions and lives according to his own set of rules. He moves in total freedom and places all the responsibilities for his life on himself. Such a life carries its own risks. People may not respect him or consider him anti-social, but this does not bother a true *swami*. He enjoys the bliss of freedom from the slavery of society and finds it so gratifying that he renounces the false respectability and hypocrisy given to him by society. This is true renunciation.

A *sannyasin* does not run away from the world or renounce society but renounces dependence on society and all its allurements, which come with golden fetters. He is like a bird on the wing — flying in the sky with wings of freedom and wisdom. Out of compassion and consciousness, he does what he can for society but never tries to fulfil anybody's expectations or gain respect to satisfy his ego.

The ego is the greatest bondage that imprisons the consciousness of the individual. It is a trap of the unconscious mind to enslave the individual. A conscious person can always choose and attain freedom from misery. Meditation is the master key to unlock the fetters of human misery.

Osho says: "Meditation brings two things — it brings wisdom; it brings freedom. These two flowers grow out of meditation. When you become silent, utterly silent, beyond the mind, two flowers bloom in you. One is of wisdom through which you know what is and what is not, and the other is of freedom, which reveals that there are no limitations on you, either of time or of space. You become liberated. Meditation is the key to liberation, to freedom to wisdom."

Great Expectations gone Kaput

Before the dawn of the new millennium there was the expectation that it would usher in a new era of non-violence, peace and prosperity. This desire arose universally in all human hearts. The world celebrated the arrival of the new millennium to leave the past behind once and for all. But this did not happen. The past made a comeback with a big bang and unleashed a rein of terror and violence. The new millennium made the depressing prophecy of despair and the spectre of the world war came alive once again.

Once again Nostradamus and other prophets of doom sprang back to life and death started doing a *tandav* in front of our eyes. Today we witness violence at our doorsteps. Not in far away USA or Afghanistan; we find ourselves surrounded by it, bathed in it. We sleep with it every night and dream of violence. It has become our breakfast, lunch and supper. We are in it. Now we are breathing it, inhaling it and exhaling it. Violence has become a fact of human life. Violence has entered deep into our unconscious, so much so that it has become one with it. Now there seems to be no escape — we are 'it'. Our past has become our present. The past millennia have become the new millennium. The animal has not yet evolved into a human being — it has simply taken a human form and is pretending to be a human being.

The enlightened sage of modern times, J. Krishnamurti,

goes deeper to say: "Violence takes many forms: not merely of brutal action or striking each other. Violence includes imitation, conformity, obedience; it exists when you pretend to be what you are not. Aggression takes many forms — polite, gentle aggressiveness with a kid glove, persuasion through affection, compelling you to think along a particular line — that is violence. Non-violence is a non-fact; not a reality. It is a projection of thought to escape from, or to accept violence and pretend that we are becoming non-violent. So, can we look at violence, free from it all — free from escape, free from ideals, free from suppression — and actually observe what violence is? When your mind is crippled by authority as it is, it is very difficult to be free and be able to look at violence."

Freedom from the brutal and violent past is only possible when we go through a deep cleansing of our unconsciousness. Meditation can bring about this metamorphosis. Osho says, "The only thing that can prevent a World War is that you start with a totally new consciousness, a new kind of humanity — a man who is capable of love, of meditation. Let love and meditation spread far and wide."

Let meditation reach as many people as possible.

Laughter Meditation for Office-goers; Nothing Official about It

People working from nine to five or even longer hours are mostly a bored lot. If we look at them, by the end of the day, we find them dull and comatose as if their entire life has been sucked out from their being.

This boredom is a universal calamity that afflicts all human beings. People seek all kinds of entertainment and still remain afflicted with this malady. It is very rare to find freshness in people's lives because they don't live a life full of good cheer, joy and ecstasy. Work feels like more of a burden than an enjoyable responsibility and sucks all the juice. It is because people don't live a life of meditation. With meditation work becomes an art and ultimately worship. Then it transforms into joy.

Osho explains: "The first thing: a meditative mind always lives in the new, the fresh. The whole existence is newly born — as fresh as a dewdrop, as fresh as a leaf coming out in the spring. It is just like the eyes of a newborn babe — everything is fresh, clear, with no dust on it. This is the first thing to be felt. If you look at the world and feel everything is old, it shows you are not meditative. When you feel everything is old, it shows you have an old mind, a rotten mind. If your mind is fresh, the world seems fresh. The question is not of the world; it is of the mirror. If there is dust on the mirror, the world looks old; if there is no dust on the mirror, how can the world be old? If things get old, you will live in boredom — everybody lives in boredom; everybody is bored to death.

"Look at people's faces. They carry life as a burden — boring, with no meaning. It seems that everything is just a nightmare, a cruel joke, a trick to torture them. Life is not a celebration; it cannot be. With a mind burdened by memory, life cannot be a celebration. Even if you laugh, your laughter carries boredom. Look at people laughing: they laugh with an effort. Their laugh may be just to be good mannered; their laugh may be out of good etiquette."

People have forgotten to have a hearty laugh. And laughter is exclusively a human quality.

Wishing you a very healthy start to your day! And remember to share this health tonic with all, without any discrimination.

No Fixed Roles

There can be no generalisation that men are from Mars and women from Venus. Both hail from both planets.

The other day people saw Kapil Dev, one of India's greatest cricketers, cry during a BBC television interview. It was not anything out of a film. It was real. People could not believe that their hero could cry like that in public, as millions of viewers watched. Newspapers and magazines published the news with a photo on the front page — it was too good an opportunity to miss.

This incident remained in the news longer than the actual controversies about Kapil's alleged involvement in match-fixing. Some people thought it was something that gave the cricketer the much-needed public sympathy. Others saw it as a weakness, for they believe that men are not supposed to express emotions. Men are expected to have no tenderness of heart, no soft feelings and should shed no tears.

This expectation is certainly very unnatural and dangerous. Nature has given man a heart and tear glands similar to those of women. But he is taught from childhood to behave like a man – and that means that he should not cry like women do. He should behave like a doughty fighter and not as a sissy girl. It is often said that boys are boys and girls are girls: it means that they should behave according to the social conditioning and not be natural.

You must have heard of the book *Men are from Mars and Women are from Venus*. Men are expected to demonstrate Martian qualities of fighting while women are expected to be tender and weep at any opportunity. This unnatural expectation has done much harm over the centuries. All the wars have been fought by men — 5,000 wars in 3,000 years. If man was also given the opportunity to weep, he would not have been as violent as he has been for thousands of years. He would have become more sensitive, poetic and also ruled by the heart. Giving too much importance to the so-called maleness and macho image has proved fatal. Man has almost forgotten to cry. He has forgotten that he has a heart, so he continues to fight as he is expected to do.

Man gave too much importance to the mind and his physical, or rather, animal instincts. As a result he proved more violent than animals. He developed technologies of mass destruction, such that he could simply press a button in a room and trigger any nuclear device. Such is the ingenuity of his mind.

Meditation is the art of striking a balance between the masculine and feminine qualities, both in men and women. It unblocks whatever has been repressed in the psyche of men and of women. The first thing that meditation does is to reconnect you with your roots and make you natural. If men need to cry, they will cry. If women have repressed their aggressiveness because of social pressures and expectation, they will need to express it in meditation and become free from it.

The fact is that both men and women are from Venus and Mars. Our social expectations categorise them and imprison them in such compartments. Consequently both become unnatural.

Meditation brings about such a forceful metamorphosis that one regains one's natural being. For the first time there is a feeling of freedom to weep or laugh according to one's natural needs.

Ask Yourself: Who am I?

Never try to be someone else and you will become mature. Maturity is in accepting the responsibility of being oneself, whatsoever the cost. Walking down the street, Mulla Nasruddin noticed a boy of about 15, smoking a cigarette.

"Aren't you a bit to young to smoke?" Mulla asked.

"Of course, I ain't," replied the lad. "I've got a girlfriend and all."

"A girlfriend?" asked Mulla.

"Yeah, picked her up last night; I did. Smashing it was."

"Good Lord! How old is she?"

"I dunno. I was too drunk to ask her."

This is no ancient joke. It's a reality, happening today with our kids. They are not even out of school or college but they are into smoking, flirting with girls, getting drunk to escape reality and consciousness, which have not even evolved. In future, we can expect more of this and worse than this. The young are already too violent as can be seen from the rise in incidents of rape. This is happening not only in the West but in India too. Why is this happening? Nobody knows. Things are no longer in our control. The East is imitating the West, and vice versa. Says Osho. "This world is a world of imitators; monkeys all. A grown-up person is one who doesn't imitate, who finds his own path, who is an individual, who looks into his own nature and asks, 'Who am I? What do I really feel'?"

Once Mulla Nasruddin's wife drove home, got out of her car and promptly fell to the ground. Mulla rushed to her help, asking, "What happened? Why did you faint?"

She replied, "It was too hot."

He asked further, "Why didn't you open the windows?"

She replied, "What! Open the windows and let the neighbors know that our car is not air-conditioned?"

People would rather die than let others know the reality. It's a prestige issue that the car must be air-conditioned, whether one can afford it or not. She preferred to keep the windows closed. She preferred to suffer than open the windows as that would have hurt her much more! So Osho says: "Nobody allows anybody to be just himself. You are conditioned to such concepts so deeply that they seem to be your own. Just relax. Forget all such concepts. Drop them like hot potatoes. It's better to be a naked tree without leaves than have plastic foliage and plastic flowers — the latter can be too ugly. Having an original face means that you aren't under the influence of any morality, religion, society, parents, teachers, priests or anyone. You live your life according to your own inner voice. You have the sensibility. You are original. The world's a great place to live in, where we are original; not copies of anything. It does not matter whether one copies Buddha, Krishna or Jesus — a copy is a copy. It is beneath human dignity to be a copy. Be original. Be your own master."

Osho asks us to meditate, "Listen to your being. It is continuously conveying hints; it is a still, small voice. It does not shout at you. And if you are silent for a while, you will start feeling your way. Be the person you are. Never try to be another, and you will become mature. Maturity is accepting the responsibility of being oneself, whatsoever the cost. Risking all to be oneself — that's what maturity is all about."

Relax to Live in Balance

Your body is your temple. Learn to communicate with it to understand what it needs. In a popular comic show on television, a candidate narrated the following joke: "A man goes to a doctor and complains of insomnia. The doctor advises him to join a call centre!" But there's a flip side to this joke. For young aspirants, call centres have ushered in a new era of prosperity and resourcefulness. Young Indians have become more American than Americans themselves. However, the bubblegum brigade has inherited more than just the American accent; they have adopted their afflictions too. They are making more money than ever before but are also getting sleeplessness and other emotional and mental problems in return. What a deal! Ancient seers would call this *maya ka chakkar*. '*Maya*' has two meanings: one, money; two, delusion. Saint Kabir has said, '*Maya maha thafini ham jaani*'. In my experience, *maya* is the greatest deceiver.

"Buddha advocated the middle path. But the young, intoxicated with sudden prosperity, do not listen. Don't get me wrong. I'm not advocating renunciation. What I'm suggesting is that even if you have to remain awake at night, practice yoga and meditation to acclimatise your body-mind-heart to the new situation. Life is always presenting new situations. The intelligent among us deal with them without getting worked up. But I find our young ones burning themselves out. The young and the restless need specific yoga and meditation techniques to deal with their sleeplessness. Staying awake is not a disease. Lord Krishna says in the *Bhagvad Gita*: 'A *yogi* remains awake while the whole world sleeps'."

The Sufis also offer prayers at night, calling it a 'night vigil' for their beloved God. Osho suggests a simple meditation method, which he calls 'The Great Nothing'. You have to be careful not to coerce the body into this, but coax it. The body is a beautiful gift from God. Before you go to sleep, sit on your chair. Be comfortable. Comfort is the most essential part of this exercise. Assume whatever posture you want. Close your eyes and relax. From your toes right up to your head, delve within to understand where you sense tension. If you feel it in your knees, relax the knees. Touch the knees and say, 'Please relax.' If you feel tension in your shoulders, tell them to relax. Within a week, you will be able to communicate with your body. By following this technique, you will discover many spots of tension and these have to be relaxed first, because if the body is not relaxed, the mind cannot follow suit. Go all over your body and shower it with love, compassion, sympathy and care. In just over five minutes you start feeling limp, almost sleepy. Now turn your consciousness to your breathing and relax it. The body is the outermost part while consciousness is the innermost; breathing is the bridge that joins them. That's why, once breathing disappears, the person dies and the bridge gets broken. Talk thus to your breath: 'Please relax. Be natural.' You will see that the moment you say this, a subtle change occurs.

Nowadays, breathing has become rather unnatural. We have forgotten to relax. We remain so tense that our breathing also seems laboured. Just tell your breathing to relax two or three times and then remain silent.

Find God in the World Around You

Modernity enriches man with such wealth, such progress that even the gods may be envious. But it also takes away beautiful qualities, which make man humane....

In the past, when a villager met a passerby, they would greet each other: "Ram, Ram!" This sounds rather primitive to the modern man, who has replaced this form of greeting of recognising God in every human being with the so-called sophisticated greetings like "good morning, good afternoon". These greetings are uttered mechanically and without any meaning, while 'Ram Ram' does have a lot of feeling. It signifies that we recognise and appreciate the divinity in every human being we encounter in life.

There's a Hasidic parable: A young man asked an old rabbi, "In the past, in the golden days, we had heard that people used to see God with their own eyes, that people used to encounter God. God used to walk on earth. God used to call people by their names. God was very close to men. What has happened now? Why is God not so close? Why can we not see him directly? Why is he hiding? Where has he gone? Why has he forgotten the earth? Why does he not hold the hands of the people stumbling in darkness? He used to do that earlier."

The old rabbi looked at the disciple and said, "My son, he is still there where he used to be, but man has forgotten how to stoop low enough to see him."

Osho explains: "Man has forgotten how to stoop. Man stands very haughtily, very proudly, very erect — separate from God. Man has become an island, no longer part of the universe. God is exactly where he used to be — he is still trying to hold your hand but you are not willing to let him. He is still confronting you but you look sideways. He is still there, calling you by your name but you are too full of your own noise, the inner talk, the continuous chattering....

"Man has forgotten to stoop, to bow down. In the course of struggling for technological progress, man has forgotten the language of the Divine. He has all the wealth at his feet and all the comforts provided by technological advancement to make him feel that he is living in heaven. But does he really live in heaven? He is more miserable than he was earlier. Why?

"Because he has become more egoistic; more haughty. He has forgotten to bow down to the Divine in every being. Otherwise it is very easy to see God, feel God, encounter God. God throbs in the heartbeat of all humans, birds and animals. He grows in the trees and plants. He flows in the waterfalls, rivers and oceans. He is spread in the rainbows around dark clouds in the vast sky. He shines in the stars, the sun and moon. One does not need to go to any temple to pray. One can sit anywhere in Nature and bow down — look within and without."

Be Original, Be Happy

When you don't long to do anything other than what you are doing, then your mind exists in the moment. Then you are at ease. Then you are in *Dharma.* In India, it is common to see interesting messages inscribed on vehicles, especially trucks. Once driving around Oregon in the US, I was amused to see a bumper sticker on a very small car: 'When I grow up, I want to be a Rolls Royce.'

I started pondering over it. This was not just a joke. It was indeed a very profound statement about human beings too. Every person in this world is unhappy or discontented with what he is; he always wants to be something, which he cannot be. Our school education also teaches us to be something; it gives us great ideals to follow. Ask any school-going child what he or she wants to become and prompt comes the answer, "I want to become Mahatma Gandhi" or "I want to become Mother Teresa".

These answers do make us happy and proud, but the fact is that life does not want carbon copies. Life believes in originals. Life, existence, God would like every human being to flower in his original manner, to become something that he, and he alone, is supposed to become. Then there's no tension. Tension arises when a rose wants to become a lotus.

Explains Osho in *The Psychology of the Esoteric*: "The

original source of all tension is in becoming. One is always trying to be something; no one is at ease with himself as he is. The being is not accepted, the being is denied, and something else is taken as an ideal to become. So the basic tension is always between that which you are and that which you long to become. You desire to become something. Tension means that you are not really pleased with what you are. Tension is created between these two. What you desire to become is irrelevant. If you want to become wealthy, famous, powerful or free, liberated, Divine, immortal, even if you long for salvation and *moksha*, the tension would be there.

"Anything that is desired as something to be fulfilled in the future, against you as you are, creates tension. The more impossible the ideal is, the more tension there will be. So a person who is a materialist is ordinarily not so tense as one who is religious, because the religious person is longing for the impossible, the far-off. The distance is so great that only a great tension can fill the gap.

"Tension means a gap between what you are and what you want to be. If the gap is more, the tension will be more. If the gap is small, the tension will be small. And if there is no gap at all, you will be satisfied with what you are. In other words, if you do not long to be anything other than what you are, your mind will exist in the moment. There is nothing to be tense about; you are at ease with yourself. You are in the Tao. To me, if there is no gap, you are religious; you are in *Dharma*."

Life: Mystery Beyond Perfection

For perfectionists, life is a puzzle to be solved. But for the wise, life is a mystery to be lived with a sense of wonder!

The wise tell us that the world is perfect as it is. You cannot ask for more. But some people are never satisfied. They want to improve things. They are so obsessed with the idea of perfection that they would improve upon God's creation too. Their obsession drives others crazy. Not only are perfectionists mad themselves, but they also drive others mad!

Here's an interesting anecdote. A king, passing through a small town, saw what he took to be an indication of amazing marksmanship. On trees, barns and fences there were many bull's-eyes, each with a bullet hole in the exact centre. He could not believe his eyes. It was almost a miracle of achievement. He himself was a good marksman and had known many great marksmen in life, but never seen anything like this. He wanted to meet the expert shot. It turned out to be a madman. "This is sensational! How in the world do you do it?" he asked the madman. "I am a good shot too, but I am nothing in front of your skill. Please tell me!"

"Easy as a pie!" said the madman, laughing uproariously. "I shoot first and draw the circles in later!"

Osho tells us not to be perfectionists. He says,

"Perfectionism is the root cause of all neurosis. Unless humanity gets rid of the very idea of perfection, it will never ever be sane. The very idea of perfection has driven the whole of mankind to a state of utter madness. To think in terms of perfection means that you are thinking in terms of ideology, goals, values, should and should-not... you have a certain pattern to fulfil, else you feel immensely guilty. And the pattern is bound to be such that you cannot achieve it. If you do achieve it, it will not be of much value to your ego!"

Perfectionism is a neurotic idea. An intelligent person will understand that life is an adventure, a constant exploration. That is its very joy! Perfection means a full stop. Perfection means ultimate death. There is no way to go beyond it. Perfectionists take life as a puzzle and look for solutions. But for the wise, life is a mystery to be lived with a sense of wonder.

Osho says, "You should be perfectly and acutely aware of the difference between a mystery and a problem. A problem is something created by the mind, but a mystery is something which is already there. A problem has some ugliness in it, like a disease. A mystery, on the other hand, is beautiful. With a problem, fights arise. Something is wrong and you have to put it right; something is missing and you must supply the missing link. With a mystery, there is no question of a fight. The moon arises at night — that is not a problem; it is a mystery. You live with it. You dance with it. You sing with it. Or you can be silent with it. Mystery surrounds you."

Hurry: A Modern Disease

Man has known many sicknesses but none so problematic as 'hurry'. Modern man is always short of time. As a matter of fact, he has no time.

Once Mulla Nasruddin went to the river to catch a boat. He was going on a journey and he was in a great hurry as he feared missing the boat. When he reached the river, he saw the boat had just left the shore. He jumped and landed on the deck, but slipped and fell in the process. His elbows were bruised, his clothes torn but he was happy — he had managed to catch the boat. He looked at his fellow travellers. Beaming with pleasure, he remarked "Well, I made it!"

One of them replied, "I don't understand, Mulla. Why all this hurry? This boat isn't going anywhere; it's just coming in to the shore!"

Hurry makes normal people blind and they cannot see which way things are moving. Down the centuries, man has known many sicknesses, but there is one sickness which was not so prevalent earlier as it is today. That special sickness is known as 'hurry'. Modern man suffers from it tremendously. He is always short of time. As a matter of fact, he has no time.

Hurry is also special because it is an imported disease, not native to India. This infectious disease has been transmitted to rich Indians by the West.

Osho explains the root cause of this disease. He says: "Western man has been living under a very wrong conception. It has created so much tension in people's minds that they can never be at ease anywhere. They are always on the go, always worried about the end; they want to do everything. But the result is just the opposite. They cannot live joyously. Everything that brings joy seems to them as a waste of time. They cannot sit silently for an hour, because their mind says to them, 'Why are you wasting the hour? You could have done this, done that.' It is because of this concept of one's life that the idea of meditation needs a very relaxed mind — no hurry, no worry, nowhere to go… just enjoying moment to moment, whatever comes."

Osho carries on: "In the Western world, they have believed death to be the end of life. In the East, we believe that we have so many lives that death is only a beautiful incident in the long procession. There will be many, many deaths. Each death is a climax of one's life, before another life begins. As the *Gita* says, 'We simply change clothes'."

Osho points out that the idea of a short life is dangerous. That's why even though the East is very poor, there is no despair, no anguish. The West is rich, but the richness hasn't brought anything to its spirituality or growth. The West is very tense. It should be relaxed for it has all the comforts at its disposal. But the basic problem is that deep down, the West knows that life is short; every moment brings it closer to death. Then, all luxuries are meaningless, because you cannot take them along. You go into death alone, all alone.

The East is relaxed. First, it does not give death any importance. Second, it is aware of its inner riches, which go with one, even beyond life. Death cannot take them away.

Spiritual Relevance of Temples

For the educated people today it has become quite fashionable to look down upon simple people who go to temples to worship or practice meditation. They consider themselves to be scientific and the temple-goers as traditional and backward. Sometimes it is seen that when these so-called rationalists suffer from a superiority complex, they become fanatics and start ridiculing temples. No matter how scientific they think themselves to be, in reality they do not understand the real science of spirituality behind the creation of temples.

Each temple in India was originally created around enlightened mystics and masters, such as Lord Buddha, Lord Mahavira, Krishna and Rama. Osho explains that since these enlightened beings were not expected to stay in one place, something more stable was needed to become the centre of life for a whole town — something around which the lives of people could be transformed. Anyone who passed by the temple received something invaluable. There was a huge magnetic field created around it and that field had a positive influence on the entire village. This is not a part of fiction because results were actually achieved. The characteristic simplicity, innocence and purity of Indian villages, which was found for thousands of years, was more due to the charged field of the temples than to the villagers themselves. However poor the village, the existence of a temple in it was absolutely necessary. Without a temple everything seemed chaotic, rhythmless.

The modern scientific world has lost something very significant which was always available to villagers in the East. Osho points out that the worst thing, which was done to destroy Eastern culture, was to destroy that charged field of the temples. Once these vibrant temples were destroyed, the entire Eastern culture crumbled. That is why today people are sceptical about the value of temples.

Osho reminds us that India cannot regain its past glory until temples come alive again. The whole alchemy of India is in its temples; it is from its temples that India received everything. There was a time when a person's life revolved around a temple.

Just as the temple gave the person a lot, the people too contributed to the temples. Unless we revive that tradition, we cannot dream of achieving greatness as a nation.

Relevance of Krishna

Indians, especially Hindus all over the world, celebrate the birthday of Lord Krishna, who is worshipped as an incarnation of God on earth — *Purnavtar*. This is not without reason. This cannot be termed blind worship or devotion. Krishna deserved it, as he is the only incarnation of God who is multi-dimensional. He is comfortable in all the shades and colours of life and he accepts life in totality — be it in love and romance or an epic war. He faces life in all its extremes — trials and tribulations, tender love and care — and celebrates everything. He leads a very colourful life and squeezes out all the juice that life has to offer. He loves life and emerges victorious. Thus he not only has a very significant message to convey, he becomes the message himself. The message becomes most effective only when it emerges from leading a real life; the life of the messenger himself. Krishna is a personification of his own message; He is the Message itself.

In his various discourses on Krishna and the *Gita*, Osho talks about the relevance of Krishna in the present moment and in the future, emphasising the need for leading a life in the totality of the moment and not being overconcerned with the result. The concern makes our energy divided and we become split. Life demands totality and authenticity.

Osho reminds us that in the *Gita*, Krishna says: "Don't

think of the result at all. It is a message of tremendous beauty, significance and truth. Don't think of the result at all. Just do what you are doing with your totality. Get lost in it. Let your creative energies flow unhindered.

"In the Divine, a Krishna-like prism, everything is accepted and transformed. But the whole thing is that it is just the same light, and what happens to your life depends on how you respond to this light.

"I give you the devil to continuously remind you that millions of people, 99 per cent, waste their lives at the first. It is a very poor life — miserable, a hell. Everybody has the destiny to reach to the fifth. Krishna has to start dancing in you; your whole life has to become a celebration. And it is not only that you give back, because when a God gives a gift to you, it doesn't look good to give the same gift back. It has to be transformed. If it comes as one light; it has to go as seven. If it comes as one single note, you have to return a whole orchestra.

"Living life in all the dimensions authentically, playfully, is the core of the message of Krishna's life. It is *raas*, an unending *raas* and his *leela*."

Osho says: "Leeladhar is one of the names of Krishna. He is the most playful God, the most non-serious; there is no comparison to Him. He is totally into life, into all dimensions of life, and He enjoys everything — from love to war, everything; there is no denial in Him. He can be good, He can be bad; He can be truthful, he can be deceitful. He can sacrifice Himself; He can cheat you. He is very spontaneous, without any ideals and without any ideology...just a man living from moment to moment, responding, not with any *a priori* idea. He has no idea of how things should be. He functions in His totality, and whatsoever happens out of that totality is good. He has no definition of goodness other than that."

THE MYSTIC REALM

永恒

This is the Buddhist alchemy: all evil can be transformed into the Bodhi path, the path to become a Buddha. Evil is not against you; you just don't know how to use it. Poison is not your enemy; you just don't know how to make medicine out of it. In wise hands poison becomes medicinal; in foolish hands medicine can become poison. It all depends on you, on your artfulness.

Transforming Emotions

Gurdjieff, a Russian mystic, was a great enlightened master of the modern times. Though he was not educated, he had several intellectual disciples, such as P.D. Ouspensky and Katherine Mansfield. Often the disciples found it hard to work with him even though they were intelligent. He would create situations to arouse all kinds of emotions in the disciples. He would create a situation where a new person would lose his/her temper, without realising that Gurdjieff had created the situation.

Osho calls it a group device. Such situations can be created, but only in a school where many people are working on themselves. And when Gurdjieff would shout, "Remember! Remain undisturbed," the participant would immediately know that this was a 'created' situation. The disturbance could not be made to disappear so suddenly because it had physical roots.

Osho explains: "Anger cannot disappear so immediately. Even now that you have come to know that you have been deceived, that no one is insulting you and no one means anything by it, it would be difficult to do anything. The anger is there; your body is filled with it, but suddenly your temperature cools down."

The anger remains only in the body. At the centre, you

cool down and you know that a point exists within you which is undisturbed. You start laughing. Your eyes are red with anger, your face is violent, but you start laughing. You know two things — a point, which is undisturbed, and a periphery, which is disturbed.

One should Feel at Home with Oneself

J Krishnamurti, the enlightened mystic, once said: "We gossip about others because we are not sufficiently interested in the process of our own thinking and our own action."

The average human being does not live more than 60 or 70 years, and what does he do during these years? Most of the time he spends gossiping, thinking and worrying about things that really don't concern him directly, such that he is left with little time to do something in his own life.

Life is really very precious and once we realise this, we will have no time for petty things. Instead, we will utilise our time in raising our own consciousness.

The Russian mystic, Gurdjieff, used to say: "We live in such a sleepy state of consciousness that if we really count the minutes we spend on being really aware, being fully conscious, it will be not more than five minutes in all the 60 years. Out of this, 20 years are spent in sleeping, while the rest of the 40 years are spent in daydreaming, fulfilling our ambitions and desires, and chasing mirages. And in the end we find really nothing in our hands."

In order to make his point, Gurdjieff cites an example. He says that we are unable to concentrate for 60 seconds on the movement of the seconds on our wristwatch — our mind tends to wander away in no time. It may take three months to reach this much concentration as our state of consciousness is forever in turmoil. And with such a disturbed state of mind, we cannot truly celebrate our life. We are not really home; we are not present in our mind though we may be physically present. The mind is in ripples and our being is not visible in these ripples.

Meditation takes us beyond these ripples, making us reach our home.

Truth Beyond Success and Failure

It does not matter to a man of awareness whether he is successful or unsuccessful, well known or absolutely unknown, powerful or a mere nobody. To a man of awareness, these dualities don't matter at all, because awareness is the greatest treasure. When you have it, you don't want anything else. You don't want to become the president or prime minister of a country.

Those who pursue power suffer even when successful — they live in the eternal fear that they might lose it any day. At first they suffer because they are not successful; later, after being successful, they suffer because of a feeling of insecurity. Moreover, they have no private space; everyone wants to meet them. There are many who are engaged in the task of 'overthrowing' them. The life of a successful man is not a life of peace.

But in failure, too, there is no peace. For a person who is aware, it is all the same. Success comes and goes, and so does failure. He remains untouched and aloof. Poet-saint Kabir sang: "I have returned to God... the 'clothing' that he had given to me to live in the world — without any change. I have not made it dirty; not even a particle of dust has gathered on it. I have put it back into his hands exactly as fresh as it was when he gave it to me."

Such is the experience of an awakened man. He lives in the darkest of nights in the same silence, in the same peace, as he lives in the brightest of days. He remains above divisions. "Such is his power, that actions can't hold him. No matter what kind of action, a Buddha transforms it." According to the Bodhidharma, a Buddha is someone who finds freedom both in good fortune and in bad.

In Greek mythology, there was King Midas, who prayed thus to God: "Just grant me one wish, that whatever I touch should turn to gold." And it seems God became tired of his continuous nagging for, after all, what are prayers if not nagging?

Finally, God granted him his wish: "Whatever you touch will turn into gold. And now leave me at peace!"

But the unconscious man cannot do anything better. Friedrich Nietzsche was right when he said that if all your prayers were fulfilled, you would be living in sheer hell. Your prayers are coming from your unconsciousness; you don't know what you are asking for.

Once his prayer was granted, Midas could not eat because whatever he touched turned into gold. He could not drink because by the time his lips touched the water, it would turn into gold. His family left him; his friends stopped coming to see him. Midas was lonely, hungry and thirsty. Midas's palace turned into gold, as did all his furniture. But to what end? He suffered despite being one of the richest men in the world.

A man of awareness, a Buddha, also has a transforming power: whatever he touches becomes blissful. When misery strikes, he finds in it something blissful; if sadness visits him, he finds something immensely beautiful and silent in it. Death comes to him but he finds only immortality in it. Whatever he touches is transformed, because now he has the transcendental perspective. And that is the greatest power in the world — not power over anybody, but simply one's own intrinsic power.

Night becomes as beautiful as day; death becomes as much a celebration as life, because the man of transcendence knows that he is eternal. There's life, there's death — he remains untouched, he remains always beyond it all. It is this quality that is the mark of an enlightened person.

The Wisdom of the Wise

Max Ehrmann, an American mystic poet, had a vision and received some profound advice. He compiled these words in his famous document: *Desiderata*. Ehrmann functioned as a medium of the Divine. Other mystics have also had similar experiences. It happened in the case of Madam Blavatsky, who wrote *The Voice of Silence*. She discovered the ancient spiritual document in the course of meditations.

Osho talks of other mystics who have had similar experiences. According to him, many parts of Friedrich Nietzsche's *Thus Spake Zarathustra* are very ancient.

The first statement in *Desiderata* says: "Hear then the wisdom of the wise: 'Go placidly amid the noise and haste, and remember what peace there may be in silence'."

Osho explains: "The wisdom of the wise seems to be tautological. Of course, wisdom can only be of the wise. What is the point of repeating it? Why say 'wisdom of the wise'? Can wisdom be of the unwise too? But there is a subtle point to be understood, because there are so many knowledgeable people in the world and the knowledgeable person appears almost as if he is wise when he is not. He speaks in the same way. The scholar who has studied the *Srimad Bhagavad Gita* his whole life speaks the same language as Krishna, but when Krishna speaks it, it is the wisdom of the wise." This is why all mystics lay emphasis on meditation and the experience of self-realisation.

Desiderata says the same: "Go placidly amid the noise and haste, and remember what peace there may be in silence."

Invitation

The inner journey of truth begins with the help of a master who has already attained the truth.

The illumination of the master becomes an invitation to the unlit lamp of the disciple who gropes in the dark, looking for somebody who can show him the way. To find such a master is really a blessing, a benediction. Half the inner journey is over on meeting such a master and the other half is over when the disciple's enlightenment comes to fruition and he becomes a master himself.

Somebody asked Osho: "Who are you?"

Osho replied: "I am an invitation. I am an invitation for all those who are seeking, searching, and have a deep longing in their hearts to find their home."

A truly enlightened master is an open invitation to one and all, without any discrimination of caste, colour or creed. He invites all to come and drink from the river of his wisdom, love and compassion and quench their thirst to seek the truth. A river does not discriminate between the deserving and the undeserving ones, but shares its water with everybody without asking for anything in return. A river simply flows and so does the enlightened master, who has become one with the infinite source of life. By sharing his light, the master does not lose anything; rather he becomes manifold. And when his disciples also become illumined, it proves the true enlightenment of the master.

The Bauls of Bengal keep singing, "*Come, beloved, come*."

Osho says that they go on sending their invitations. Love is nothing but an opening, a receptivity, a welcome, an invitation to say, 'I am ready; come, please.'

There is a beautiful statement by Mevlana Jalaluddin Rumi, one of the greatest Sufi masters ever: "Come, come, whoever you are; wanderer, worshipper, lover of learning...it does not matter. Ours is not a caravan of despair. Come, even if you have broken your vow a thousand times, come, come, yet, again come. Come, come, whoever you are...sinner, unconscious, living a life which is not glorious, divine, meaningful; living a life which has no poetry, no joy, a life of hell...whosoever you are, Mevlana says, 'Come, I am ready to receive you. Be my guest!' The master is a host; he refuses nobody."

True masters never refuse anybody. They cannot. If they start refusing people, there is no hope. If you go under a tree, a shady tree — tired after your journey and the burning sun on your head — does the tree refuse you, does not give you refuge, does not shelter you? This never happens. The tree is always ready to give you shelter, its shadow, its fruit, its flowers and its fragrance.

Guru, the Physician of Life

India celebrates *Ashadh Purnima,* the full moon of July as *Guru Purnima.* It is the day when all disciples come together to express their gratitude towards their *guru.* This is something uniquely Indian. It is unlike a student-teacher relationship, which is very formal. A teacher imparts knowledge to students and gets paid for it. A *guru* does not merely impart knowledge to his disciples, he shares even his being and enlightenment with them. This way the disciples learn the deeper meaning of life by living in the *guru's* presence. The *guru* need not teach with his words; he guides with his own life. Hence a teacher does not command the same love and respect that a *guru* does; a teacher does not deserve it.

Teachers often complain that their students are not as respectful to them as they should be. Respect cannot be forcibly demanded; it has to be natural and arise naturally. When a teacher evolves into a *guru,* he commands natural respect; not just respect, but love and devotion too. The disciple becomes so devoted to the *guru* that he can willingly sacrifice his life for him, though a true *guru* never expects any sacrifice. The *guru* shares his being, his love and light with his disciples unconditionally.

Something about the meaning of the word *guru* — *gu* means 'darkness' and *ru* means 'dispeller'. One who dispels darkness is your *guru.* The first basic requirement for living with a *guru* is meditation. Meditation does not involve a few deep-breathing exercises; it is a way of life. Meditation is the medicine for all social sicknesses that people suffer from. That's why these two words — meditation and medicine — have the same root, '*medi*'. The *guru* gives the medicine of meditation to his disciples and makes them healthy. Talking about this health, Osho explains the Sanskrit word for healthy, which is *swastha*. *Swa* means 'self' and *stha* means 'rooted'. You become healthy when you become rooted in your self. You are sick when you lose connection with your self, your own being. Meditation reconnects you with your self and makes you healthy. That's why it can be called medicine.

Meditation is the panacea for all ailments. It is the art of living a really healthy life. Buddha calls himself a *vaidya*. Guru Nanak says the same. All enlightened persons of the East do not call themselves philosophers, they call themselves physicians. They are not ordinary doctors. They are physicians of the inner dimension. They cure the sickness of the mind. Buddha says, "Don't ask me silly questions of philosophy; I am not a philosopher. Tell me about your real sickness and I will give you the cure. Let me uproot your sickness."

Basically, a man of enlightenment makes our vision brighter by removing dust from our eyes. He teaches us the method of cleaning the mirror of our mind and leading our life with clarity. Meditation is nothing else but clarity; it is a way of living our life in total awareness. It is not that we pray or meditate for a few minutes in the day and then continue living life unconsciously in the regular mechanical manner. No, meditation is moment-to-moment awareness. It remains there all the time — it becomes 'us'. Meditation is an intelligent response to the moment.

The Grip of Habits: Theory of *Karma*

The way we live our life is not a conscious way of living. We live a mechanical life propelled by our habits. It is the easiest way to live, but it makes life dull.

We do feel cosy and comfortable but our level of consciousness starts receding. Sharpness in our life comes when we bring more and more awareness to each moment. We are able to get out of the vicious circle of habits and liberate ourselves from *karmic* bondage.

The theory of *karma* exists, but only for those who live life without full awareness. For a man of awareness, like the Buddha, this theory has no relevance.

Osho often told the story of a Hindu mystic, Eknath, who embarked on a year-long pilgrimage, to visit all the sacred places of the country. A thousand people travelled with him.

A thief in one town came and said to him, "I know that I am a thief and not worthy enough to be a member of your group, but do give me a chance. I would like to come for the pilgrimage."

Eknath replied, "It will be difficult because one year is a long time and you may start stealing people's things. You may cause trouble. Please drop this idea."

But the thief was insistent. He said, "For one year I will stop stealing, but I must come. And I promise you that for one year I will not steal a single thing from anybody."

Eknath agreed reluctantly.

But within a week trouble started. Things started disappearing from people's luggage, and what was even more puzzling was that things would disappear from somebody's bag only to be found in somebody else's.

The man in whose bag they would be found would say, "I really don't know how these things came into my bag."

One night Eknath, pretending to be asleep, lay awake, keeping a vigil. In the middle of the night, the thief started changing things from one person's luggage to another person's. Eknath caught him red-handed and asked, "What happened to your promise?"

The thief replied, "I have not stolen a single thing. But this is my old habit. In the middle of the night if I don't do some mischief, it is impossible for me to sleep. And for one year, not to sleep? Be kind, I am not stealing; things are just getting exchanged from one person to another. And moreover, after one year I have to start stealing again, so it will be a good practice for me."

Similarly we too are victims of our habits. Hindus call it the theory of *karma*: each action that we repeat, or each thought — because thought is also a subtle action in the mind — becomes more and more powerful. Then we are caught in its vice-like grip.

We get imprisoned in the habit. When we get angry, we rationalise and say that the situation demanded it. That's how our ego goes on assuming. We feel we are still the boss, but we are not. Anger comes out of old habits, out of the past. And when anger comes, we try to find an excuse for it.

Osho points out, "Nobody is responsible except you.

Nobody can make you angry, and nobody can make you happy. You become happy on your own; you become angry on your own, and you become sad on your own. Unless you realise this, you will always remain a slave. Our relationships are creating miseries for us for the simple reason that we lack awareness; our behaviour makes us come out of unconsciousness and we become more and more conscious to make life blissful."

Flow with the River of Life

All of us want to connect with the ultimate truth, but the real trick lies in realising that Buddha resides within us. We are all seekers, always looking for something. We are never content with what we have in us or with us. For us, something is always missing. Living on this earth, we yearn for a paradise somewhere.

Osho narrates a Chinese allegory about a monk in search of Buddha.

After travelling for many years, the monk arrived in the country where Buddha lived. A river flowed in between, preventing him from meeting the Buddha. He inquired for a ferry or a boat to reach the other shore. But the people informed him that nobody would take him there as it was believed that whoever went to the other shore, never returned. Thus the only alternative was to swim across. Afraid, of course, because the river was very wide but with no other way out, the monk started swimming. In the middle of the river, he saw a corpse floating and drawing near him. He tried in many ways to dodge it, but could not. Finding no way to escape from it, he swam towards the corpse. He looked at the face. He couldn't believe his eyes — it was his own corpse! And then the corpse floated away. All that he had learnt, all that he had possessed — ego, the centre of his mind, the self — everything seemed to be floating away with the corpse. He could feel no need to go to the other shore. He began to laugh, because he had been searching for the Buddha and all this while, Buddha lay within him. He returned to the shore he had left a few moments ago, but people failed to recognise him. He told them, "I am the same man!"

But he was not. Everybody had come back, but everyone had changed. Osho says: "If you really go on journeying towards the Buddhaland endlessly to know the Ultimate, some day or the other you will come to the wide river where all that you have done, all that you can do, all that you have possessed, all that you can possess, all that you have been, all that you can be, all is taken away by the wide river. You are left alone, with no possessions, no body, no mind. In that aloneness, flowers the flower of Buddha. You have reached the Buddhaland. You have come to know the Tao."

Osho adds: "If you can flow with the river of life, suddenly you will see your own corpse flowing down the river — all past, all learning and all possessions gone. There is only the pure simple being, and that is what it is to be the Buddha. If you float with the river, sooner or later you will come to encounter your corpse. If you fight with the river, it will never happen. And blessed is the man who has seen his own corpse flowing down the river of life."

Take the Decision to be Happy

Humans are conscious beings who can decide how they want to live. It is only the animals who have no choice and cannot decide. A donkey needs to be driven in some direction for work; else it would simply stand around or wander aimlessly. Cows, buffaloes, bulls, camels and dogs, all can be tamed for they don't have much choice. The Hindi word for animals, *pashu*, originates from *pash*, meaning 'bondage'. So, a *pashu* is one who is in bondage. When humans behave as if they are in bondage, they are no better than animals. With evolution comes consciousness, freedom, choice and the ability to make sane decisions. One sane decision is to remain happy. To some extent, being happy is our choice. We can assess the reasons for our unhappiness and avoid them. These reasons usually are jealousy, anger, ego, greed and stupid desires that cannot be fulfilled. Osho suggests: "One should look not for happiness but for the causes of suffering, and ways to overcome it. The moment you are out of suffering, there is happiness. Happiness isn't something you have to wait for. You can wait till infinity and happiness may not come to you, unless you destroy the cause of suffering."

Look around and see what makes you unhappy — jealousy, anger, an inferiority complex; what is it? Here's the miracle: if you can enter your suffering as a meditation, to the deepest roots, you can make it disappear by just observing. You needn't do anything more. If you find the authentic cause by observing, the suffering will disappear. If it doesn't disappear, it means you are not observing deep enough.

Osho recounts an interesting anecdote from the life of Mulla Nasruddin. A very rich man wanted to be happy. He tried all the means at his disposal, but nothing worked. He visited many saints but not one could help him. Then someone suggested that he consult Nasruddin. The rich man took a bagful of diamonds, and showed it to Nasruddin, who sat beneath a tree outside the town, resting in the sun. The man said: "I am very miserable. I want happiness. I have not tasted happiness even once, and death is approaching. Can you help me? I am ready to give anything for it. How can I be happy? I have all kinds of things that the world can give, yet I am unhappy. Why?"

Nasruddin looked at the man. Then he suddenly jumped up, snatched the bag and ran. Of course, the man followed him, crying and shouting, "I've been cheated, robbed!"

Nasrudding knew the streets well, so he went zigzagging across town. The rich man had never run in his life. As he ran, tears streamed down his face and he kept wailing: "I've been robbed. Totally robbed. Those were my entire life's earnings. Save me, people. Help me!"

A crowd began to follow him. By the time they caught up with Nasruddin, he was back at the spot where the rich man had found him first — under the tree, sunning himself. The rich man was crying. When Nasruddin returned his bag, he exclaimed, "Thank God!" And tears of joy ran down his face, and peace overcame him.

Nasruddin pointed out, "Look, I made you happy. Now, do you know what happiness is? This bag has been with you for years, yet you were unhappy. It had to be taken away from you to teach you how to be happy."

Synthesis Produces a Beautiful Organic Unity

Once Osho was asked: "Is it right to say that movements in the West like Arica, Zen, Sufism, EST and TM are an inevitable synthesis of Eastern mysticism and Western science?"

Osho replied: "East and West are polarities. If you try to synthesise them — take something of the East and something of the West and make a hotchpotch out of it — it will be a compromise; not a synthesis. It will be mechanical, not organic. You can put things together — that is a mechanical unity — but you cannot put a tree together, you cannot put a human being together. The unity of a tree grows; it comes from its innermost core, spreading towards its circumference. It arises in the centre. A mechanical unity can be put together from the outside: you can put a car or a clock together; but they have neither a centre nor a soul.

"It is a unity put together from the outside. It works; it is utilitarian. But a tree, a bird, a human — you cannot put them together. They grow. Their unity comes from their innermost core. They have a centre.

"A compromise is a mechanical unity; a synthesis is an organic growth. So whatever is happening in the name of EST, TM or Arica, is mechanical unity.

"The greatest danger is that the East has developed great insight into religion and the West, great insight into science. When a person from the West starts searching in the East, his attitude is scientific.

"He can understand only that which is scientific in the East. Eastern science is rudimentary. When a religious person from the East goes to the West, he looks into Western religion, which is very rudimentary. And he can understand only religious language.

"Now what is happening? East and West are meeting in Arica, EST, TM, and other so-called spiritual movements but just the opposite of what was expected is happening. It is not Eastern religion meeting Western science; it is Eastern science meeting Western religion."

Osho warns against creating a synthesis of the religions of the world. He says: "Read the *Qur'an*, the *Vedas*, the *Bible*, the *Dhammapada* and find the similarities but the *Qur'an* is beautiful only because of those things which are not in the *Gita*.

"Beauty is in uniqueness; similarities become clichés. They become meaningless and monotonous. The Himalayas are beautiful because they have something unique that is not in the Alps. And the Ganges is beautiful because it has something that is not in the Amazon.

"Of course, both are rivers; there are many similarities, but if you look deep for similarities, you will live in a boring world.

"Go into your innermost being. If you go beyond the object, you have gone beyond the West; if you go beyond the subject, you have gone beyond the East.

"Then the transcendental arises; the synthesis is there. When it has happened within you, you can spread it without also.

"The synthesis has to happen within human beings, not in books, dissertations, Ph.D. theses. An organic unity is possible only in an organic way."

One Bubble to the Other: 'Thank You so Much!'

Osho was asked why he didn't write his autobiography. Osho replied: "All autobiographies are ego-biographies. It is not the story of the soul. As long as you do not know what the soul is, whatever you write is ego-biography."

Neither Jesus, nor Krishna, nor Buddha had written their autobiographies. Writing or speaking about oneself has not been possible for those who have known themselves, because after knowing, the person changes into something so formless that we call it the facts of his life — facts like date of birth, events — all dissolve.

They cease to have any meaning. The awakening of the soul is so cataclysmic that once it occurs, when you open your eyes you find that everything is lost.

Once you know your soul, an autobiography is only a dream-like version of oneself, like writing an account of your dreams. Such writing has no more value than a fantasy, a fairy tale. So it is difficult for an awakened person to write.

On becoming awakened and aware, he finds that there is nothing worth writing. It is all a dream. The experience of becoming aware remains, but what is known through the experience cannot be written down. Reducing such an experience to words makes it seem insipid and absurd. A dying Buddha was asked: "Where will you go after death?"

He said, "I have been nowhere, so where can I go after death?"

The meaning of Buddhahood is 'nowhereness'. One is nowhere, so the question of being somewhere does not arise. If you can be quiet and silent, only breathing remains like air inside a bubble.

When there are no thoughts, there is nothing but breathing. So Buddha says, "I was only a bubble. Where was I? A bubble has burst and you are asking where it has gone."

One day Lin Chi ordered the removal of all Buddha idols. When asked the reason for doing so, he said: "As long as I was thinking that I am, I believed that Buddha was. But when I myself am not there, when I am only an air bubble, then I know that someone like Buddha also could not have been there."

In the evening Lin Chi was again worshipping Buddha idols. When asked the reason for it, he said: "I was helped in my own non-being by Buddha's non-being. That is why I am giving thanks. It was a thanksgiving from one bubble to another, nothing more."

An autobiography does not survive. Deeply speaking, the soul itself does not survive. So far we have understood only that the ego does not survive. For thousands of years, we have been told that the ego does not survive when one attains self-knowledge.

But to put it correctly, the soul itself does not survive. Buddha said, "The soul also does not survive; we become non-soul."

Mahavira talked only of the death of the ego; that much could be understood. It is not that Mahavira did not know that even the soul does not survive, but he had in mind our limited understanding. Therefore, he spoke only of giving up the ego, knowing that the soul would automatically dissolve.

The idea of the soul is a projection of the ego. But Buddha revealed the secret which had been closely guarded for so long. That created difficulties. If the soul does not survive either, they said, then everything is useless.

Where are we? Buddha was right. Everything is like a dream sequence, like the rainbow colours formed on a bubble. The colours die when the bubble bursts.

Go Ahead, Make a Face

Gurdjieff was a Russian master with mysterious ways of relating to people, such that each disciple who wrote about him described him differently. Everybody who met him would carry away the image of either a good man or a rascal, and many were the arguments on this subject.

Osho called Gurdjieff a master of changing faces. He had become so efficient at this that the disciple to his right would feel one thing, while the one to his left would feel differently. With the left of his face, he would show love, and with the other, anger. And outside, one disciple would say, "What a loving man," while the other would say, "he is under some illusion; he was so angry!" Such mastery is beautiful. It is said that no one had ever seen Gurdjieff's real face, because he was always acting. He would show you the face you needed to see; never the face that was not needed by you.

Gurdjieff enjoyed it tremendously. He did it as a reminder that we live in a fake world, where one has to keep changing faces according to the situation. It is possible to recall one's original face only through meditation. He said, "To me, and to the *Upanishads*, right conduct means just the right rules of behaviour with others.

"You are not going to be here forever. You cannot change the world; you cannot change everybody; you can at the most change yourself. So it is better to change yourself inwardly. Don't be in a continuous fight with everybody. Faces are helpful to avoid fights, unnecessary struggles, because that dissipates energy. Preserve your energy for inner work. And that work is so significant that it needs all the energy you can give to it."

For the outside world, remain an actor, and don't think of this as deceit. If children like toys to play with, you are not deceiving them by not giving them a real gun; let them play with the toy gun. Look at the other and at what he needs. Give out of consideration for him. This is all that is meant by right conduct.

No Distractions

Osho tells a Tibetan story. A Lama, who worked in a valley far away wrote a letter to the chief of his monastery: 'We need one Lama here.'

The chief called his disciples and said, "I'd like to send five of you."

One asked, "But only one has been asked for. Why five?"

The chief said, "You will know. I will send five and hope that one will reach because the way is long, and the distractions a thousand and one."

They laughed and thought, 'The old man has lost his mind. Why send five when one is needed?' But the chief insisted, so off they went.

The next morning, as they passed a village, a messenger from the headman came running to them, "Our priest has died and we need one. The salary is good."

The village looked prosperous, so one of the five said, "I'd like to stay because this too is Buddha's work. Why go to the valley? There too I'm going to do the same work. The four of you will be enough. Anyway, only one is needed! I'll stay here." Thus one dropped out.

The next day, as they passed by the outskirts of a town, the king encountered them. One young monk was healthy, handsome and radiant. The king said, "Wait! I'm looking for a young man to marry my daughter. You seem to be just right. Are you ready? I have only one daughter. My whole kingdom will be yours."

Of course, the young man said to his friends: "Goodbye!" The second thus dropped out.

Now the other three realised that the old chief was not mad. The way was long and the distractions many! They decided, "We will not do such a thing." But deep down they were jealous that one of them had become a king and another a great priest.

The third night, they lost their way. From a faraway hilltop, only one lamp could be seen in a house. Somehow they reached it. There was only a young woman present, who said, "It is good that you have come. You are a Godsend because my parents were to come back this evening but haven't. I was afraid to be alone in this house, so far away from town. You have been sent by the Buddha himself. Please stay with me. Don't leave me until my parents return."

Next morning it was time for them to leave. But one of them had fallen in love with the woman and said, "I cannot go until her parents are back. That would not be compassion, but *passion*! To leave her alone won't be virtuous. Buddha will never forgive me. I'll stay." And so, the third lama dropped out too.

In a village, the next morning, the remaining two were surrounded by a crowd of people. They were challenged by an atheist scholar in the village: "You have to prove that what Buddha says is true."

One accepted. The second said, "What are you doing? Who knows how long it will go on?"

The first said, "Even if my whole life is wasted, I'm devoted to Buddha, and this man has challenged Buddha's philosophy." It was not a challenge to Buddha but to his ego.

"I cannot leave this village, I will convert it. You go. In fact, only one is needed there." Thus, the fourth dropped out.

Only one reached the destination!

Hell and Heaven

What is hell and what is heaven — geographical places above or below the earth or psychological spaces in and around our minds?

Osho says: "No! Hell is being out of step with Nature; heaven is being in step with Nature. And that is the hidden harmony. If you can find it, you are in bliss. If you cannot, you are miserable. Nobody else is responsible."

He illustrates this through a beautiful story. Once, a Rabbi came to a village on his horse on his way to another town. He was very tired and wanted a little rest, so he went into an inn, leaving his horse under a tree outside, with some hay for it to eat. Mulla Nasruddin was sitting under another tree, drunk. The horse was beautiful. He approached it just to admire it. As he stood near the horse, a man passed by; he was a merchant of horses. The merchant asked Nasruddin, "Is this your horse?"

Drunk, and feeling very good that such a beautiful horse belonged to him, he said, "Yes."

The merchant asked, "I would like to purchase your horse. How much would you like to take for it?"

Now Nasruddin was caught. He quoted an impossible price. So he said, "Two thousand rupees."

The horse was not worth more than 500 rupees. But it

so happened that the merchant said, "Here, take these 2,000 rupees."

Now, Nasruddin was in real trouble. Two thousand rupees! He thought: 'The Rabbi is inside and he doesn't know. Why not take the 2,000 rupees? Nobody is looking, so there should be no problem at all.' So he said, "Okay." He took the money; the merchant took the horse.

The moment the horse was gone, the Rabbi emerged from the inn. Nasruddin was in a dilemma over what to do now with the money and as it is he was too drunk to make a quick getaway. Thinking hard, he found a solution. He leaned down on all fours as if he were a horse and put some hay into his mouth. The Rabbi couldn't believe what he saw. He said, "What are you doing? Are you mad?"

Nasruddin said, "First, listen to my story." Now his mind was working really fast. He had become a theologian: now he was working out one answer, then another question, but then he got caught in his own trap. He said, "Nearly 20 years ago, when I was a young man, I committed a sin with a woman. What did God do? He was so angry that he punished me and turned me into a horse — your horse, Rabbi! And for 20 years, I served you but it seems the punishment is over and I'm restored to being a man."

The Rabbi started to tremble on seeing that a sinner had been punished. Who is not a sinner after all? The Rabbi himself had sinned with several women, so this phenomenon created fear in him. He fell down on his knees and started praying. But then, there was a practical problem to be solved. He said, "All this is okay but I have to go to another town. How will I?"

Nasruddin suggested, "The market is not very far. You can go and find a horse."

So off the Rabbi went to the market, and there found his own horse standing at the horse merchant's place! He could not believe his eyes. He started trembling again. He went to the horse and whispered into its ear, "What, Nasruddin! So soon again?"

The mind keeps on playing tricks, creating gods, praying, being punished, being sent to hell and heaven...the whole process is of the imagination. There is no hell, no heaven; only you are there and so is existence, as also energy — infinite energy. If you are with it, it is with you.

You have to stop imagining. You have to feel that misery comes when you are out of step with Nature, and happiness comes when you are not out of step.

Accept Life, Thank Life

We consider ourselves wise. In fact, we are sure that we are so. But do we know that a higher and deeper wisdom exists? It flows in life's vastness. It is intrinsic to existence.

When we express our desire and it does not get fulfilled, we start wondering why this life does not fulfil our desires! We pray to God, to our deities. We start expecting that through prayers our desires will be fulfilled. It may happen and it may not. When this does not happen, we are disappointed. This leads to misery.

Well, this way, we are really being unwise. Life is not obliged to fulfil all our desires. Life gives us what we really need. It follows its own wisdom, unknown to us. When we accept this, we stop complaining because our hearts fill with gratitude to life. Acceptance gives us happiness. For a truly religious man, total acceptance of whatever life brings is real prayer. He does not impose any demands or expectations on life. He lives in a state of 'let go'.

In his discourse on *The Sword and the Lotus*, Osho tells the story of a Sufi mystic, Junnaid, who, in every evening prayer, thanked existence for its compassion, love and care.

Once, Junnaid was travelling. For three days, he and his disciples went from village to village, but people everywhere were very hostile and turned against Junnaid. They thought his teachings were not exactly the teachings of Mohammed. His teachings seemed to be his own. They said, "He is corrupting the people." So from these villages, they got no food; not even water.

On the third day, they were in a really bad shape. His disciples thought, 'Now let us see what happens in the prayer. How can he now say to existence, 'You are compassionate to us. You love us. You care about us. We are grateful to you?' But when prayer-time came, Junnaid prayed as usual. After the prayer, his followers said, "This is too much. For three days, we have suffered hunger and thirst. We are tired; we have not slept and still you are thanking existence and telling it that it takes so much care of us that we are grateful to it!"

Junnaid said, "My prayer does not depend on any condition. Those things are ordinary. Whether I get food or not, I don't want to bother existence about it. Such a small thing in such a big universe! If I don't get water, even if I die, it does not matter. My prayer will remain the same. Because to this vast universe, it makes no difference whether Junnaid is alive or dead."

Osho explains: "This is what I mean when I say that don't take anything seriously; not even yourself. And then you will see that anger simply has not happened. Anger is certainly one of the great leakages of our spiritual energy. If you can manage to be playful about your desires, and still be the same whether you succeed or fail, you will be happy. Start thinking about yourself at ease — not that you are meant to be victorious; not that you have to succeed always in every situation. This is a big world and we are small people. Once this settles into your being, then everything is acceptable. Anger disappears, and the disappearance brings a new surprise, because when anger disappears, it leaves behind tremendous energy of compassion, love and friendship.

When the Blind Lead the Blind

The search for truth makes us look for a *guru* who can guide us in the right direction. But can we be sure that the *guru* knows where the truth lies?

Today, so many people feel frustrated and hopeless in their life that they are in a rush to find someone who can give them a *mantra* of hope, of happiness. Such people end up with pseudo-masters. Ninety per cent of these so-called *gurus* are not real masters; they are pretenders. But they have a huge following, thanks to the television where anyone can spend money and attract large crowds with false promises. This is the greatest crime in the name of religion and spirituality. About such people, Guru Nanak had said: "*Andha andha thelia, dono koop pedant*" (The blind leads the blind and both fall into the ditch.)

Osho narrates a beautiful incident from Nanak's life. The enlightened master was passing through Lahore. A pseudo-mystic, a false Sufi, a pretender in the city had a great following. When he saw Nanak, he became scared, though there was nothing to be afraid of. Nanak was alone with his disciple Mardana. Mardana would play a musical instrument and Nanak would sing. They were innocent people.

An informer told the pseudo-teacher: "A great master has come. He is staying outside the city and many people have already started visiting him." The pseudo-Sufi was worried. He sent a cupful of milk, so full you couldn't put another drop into it, to Nanak.

The disciple who had to take it to Nanak said, "What does this mean?"

The pseudo-Sufi said, "You don't worry about the meaning. Take it to Nanak and let us see what happens."

Nanak was offered the cup and told, "The Sufi master sends his salutations to you."

Nanak told Mardana, "Just there, nearby are wild flowers growing. Pick one." Mardana couldn't understand what was happening. Nanak put that wild flower in the cup and gave it back to the messenger. All he said was, "Take this to your master."

Again, he said, "But I don't understand!"

Nanak said, "Your master will."

The Sufi had sent the cupful of milk to say: "Here, there is no need for any other master. The place is full of Sufis. You are not welcome — go elsewhere!"

But Nanak floated a flower in the cup, to say: "You need not be worried about me. I will not disturb anything. Even in a full cup, I will simply float like a flower. I am above — you need not worry. You can continue your shop, I will not take away your customers."

The Sufi was completely exposed to his disciples, because they could compare the two. They sat with Nanak and immediately, as if an arrow had penetrated their being, a strange joy arose within them. It had never happened in the presence of that so-called Sufi. Soon, he himself came to Nanak to beg forgiveness.

Nanak said, "Who am I to forgive you? Ask forgiveness from existence itself. You have been deceiving thousands, delaying their enlightenment. Your crime is great, though nobody will call it a crime because it is so invisible."

Be Grateful to All

Why are we always angry? The root of anger is usually our discontentment with situations or with people. We are angry when we find that others are not fulfilling our expectations. Buddha made a very strange statement: "In your anger, you punish yourself for somebody else's fault." It looks very strange the first time you read it, but it's true. In this world, nobody can really fulfil the other's expectations fully and people will naturally be angry. It happens even if you are a Buddha.

Osho tells a beautiful story. When Buddha became enlightened, his first thought was to return to his kingdom. If his father were still alive, Buddha owed him something — he was his only son while he himself had given him immense suffering. Buddha was to be his support in old age, his successor — but he had escaped. So his first thought was to convey his own ecstasy to his father.

But he was unaware that his father would not be able to recognise him as a Buddha. His inner eye was not open. He thought only through the mind; he did not know any approach through the no-mind. When Buddha faced the old man, he was really angry. He said, "You deceived me in my old age. Where have you been for twelve years? What is this nonsense — an emperor's son carrying a begging bowl! Astrologers had predicted that you would become a world conqueror, but you have chosen this stupid life!"

Buddha stood silently. He wanted to let the man give vent to his anger first.

The old man saw, after half an hour, that while he had been shouting and abusing and condemning, his son was simply standing there silently, absolutely unperturbed. He looked closely.

Buddha said, "Look closely. I'm not the man who left you; that man died long ago. Yes, I'm in the same continuity but the earlier one was mud; while now I'm the lotus. Don't take revenge against the lotus because you are angry with the mud. Let me wash your tears (because the old man was full of tears now) and clean your eyes. Cool down. Look, I'm not the man who left the palace. I'm transformed. I left as a mortal, I return as an immortal. I left as an ordinary human, I return as Divine."

The father looked at him — certainly there was a great change. For a few moments, there was utter silence. Something transpired between father and son, and the father said, "Forgive me. In my anger, with my tears, with my old eyes, I couldn't recognise the transformation. Now my only desire is that you initiate me on the same path that transforms mud into lotus."

Nothing was said, and the father got initiated.

Osho concludes: "Everybody is creating a space for you to be transformed — even those who think they are obstructing you or whom you think to be your enemies. Your friends, enemies, good people and bad, favourable circumstances and hostile — together they create the context in which you can be transformed and become a Buddha. Be grateful to all."